GLOBE
READING
COMPREHENSION
PROGRAM

BEGINNINGS

GLOBE BOOK COMPANY
Englewood Cliffs, New Jersey

Contributing Writers:
Linda Schechet Tucker
Margery E. Bernstein

Consultants:

Miriam Folk
Director of Reading, Carlisle Area School District, Carlisle, PA

Cynthia Martin
Reading Specialist, Palos Verdes Estates, CA

Robert J. Scaffardi
English Department Chairperson/Area Coordinator, Cranston High School East,
Cranston, RI

Elaine Healy
Teacher Consultant, Clark County School District, Las Vegas, NV

Maryellen Rafferty
Reading Teacher, East Meadow School District, East Meadow, NY

Sharon Sidone
Reading Teacher, First Colonial High School, Virginia Beach, VA

Photo research: Ann Levy

Cover illustration: William A. Giese

Photo Acknowledgments: UPI/Bettmann Newsphoto: 2, 10, 28, 30, 34, 58, 62, 102,
112; The Bettmann Archive: 14, 56, 88, 106, 108, 122, 130; Reuters/Bettmann
Newsphotos: 26; AP/Wide World Photos: 38, 74, 86, 96, 104, 132; © Burk Uz-
zle/Archive Pictures: 46; © Gordon S. Smith/Photo Researchers: 64; © Sandra Man-
si/Gamma-Liaison: 70; © Nancy Pierce/Photo Researchers: 82; © Joel Gordon 1979:
128; © Suzan Oristaglio/Photo Researchers: 134; Jerome Wexler/Photo Researchers:
142; © John Eastcott and Yva Momatuik/The Image Works 144; UFS, Inc.: 33, 137;
Courtesy of Vermont Historical Society: 78; Cordier & Ekstrom Inc.: 84; Courtesy
Dept. Library Services-American Museum of Natural History: 121; Ski for Light,
Courtesy American Foundation for the Blind, New York: 98.

Illustrators:
Eldon Doty: 4, 17, 22, 41, 42, 54; Thomas Sperling: 6, 81, 94, 97, 100, 110, 112;
Mark Stein Studios: 8, 37, 61; Richard Martin: 18, 20, 48; Bradford Brown: 24, 50;
Hrana L. Janto: 66, 68, 69, 136; Liane Fried: 77, 88, 124; Gary Tong: 72, 118; Lane
Yerkes: 90, 92, 93, 114, 116, 117, 126, 138, 140.

Globe Book Company
A Division of Simon & Schuster
Englewood Cliffs, New Jersey

ISBN: 1-55675-006-4

PRINTED IN THE UNITED STATES OF AMERICA   10 9 8 7 6 5 4 3

CONTENTS

INTRODUCTION

Reading is like a new beginning each time you pick up a book. When you read, you want to learn about different places and meet new and exciting people. With each person you meet and place you visit, you become more curious about the people and world around you.

In this book, you'll read six different kinds of selections. Here's a sample of what you'll find.

NEWS: In these selections, you'll find stories like those you read in newspapers or magazines. For example, you'll read about the 11-year-old boy who piloted an airplane across the country.

HISTORY: People and places of the past are the subject of these selections. One selection takes you to the ancient Inca Empire in South America.

BIOGRAPHY: Here you'll find the real-life stories of some famous and interesting people, such as Florence Nightingale, the founder of the nursing profession.

SCIENCE, TECHNOLOGY, IDEAS: If you're interested in science and the inventions that science makes possible, you'll enjoy the selection about the world's largest telescope and what it tells scientists about the universe.

FICTION: This category features selections about imaginary characters and events. You'll read about Anansi, a character in Jamaican folklore.

NATURE, MARVELS, MYSTERIES: In these selections, you'll discover two kinds of marvels and mysteries—those found in nature and those created by people. For example, you'll understand why your hands are made the way they are. You will also read about why a year does not always have 365 days.

This book is organized in a helpful way. Each lesson begins with an introduction and two questions. Think carefully about the questions. Words in the selection that may be unfamiliar to you are defined at the bottom of the page. They are also included in a glossary at the back of this book. After each selection are questions and activities that will help you to become a more thoughtful reader.

So turn the page to begin a new experience in reading.

CROSS-COUNTRY FLYER

You know that an 11-year-old isn't allowed to drive a car. However, an 11-year-old from Arlington, Texas, flew a plane across the country.

● Have you ever taken an airplane trip?

● What do you think it feels like to fly an airplane?

John Kevin Hill did more than wish he could be a pilot. On June 24, 1987, he took off from an airport in Los Angeles, California. He was the pilot of a Cessna 210. Seven days later, he landed at National Airport in Washington, D.C. John Kevin had piloted a small plane for 2,500 miles!

John Kevin first took flying lessons when he was nine years old. He loved the feeling of flying right from the start. He did have a problem seeing out of the plane, but sitting on two pillows took care of that.

Because John Kevin is so young, he is not allowed to fly alone. It is against the law for anyone under 16 to fly solo. An adult pilot must always be on board. John Kevin's flying teacher, Mike Fields, flew across the country with him. Mike had his own set of controls. He could have taken over the plane at any time if something had gone wrong. But nothing ever did. John Kevin was the pilot all the way from Los Angeles to Washington, D.C.

Now that John Kevin has flown cross-country, what does he plan to do next? He wants to fly around the world in 1989. After that, he hopes to become an astronaut. John Kevin really wants to go to the moon. He just might do it!

pilot (PY lut)   a person who operates an airplane
piloted (PY lut id)   acted as pilot; operated an airplane
solo (SOH loh)   alone
controls (kun TROHLZ)   the system for operating an airplane
astronaut (AS truh naut)   a person who is trained to fly a spaceship

2

Direct Recall

Circle the letter of the choice that best completes each sentence.

1. John Kevin Hill flew from Los Angeles, California, to
   a. Washington, California.   **b.** Washington, D.C.   **c.** Cessna, California.

2. John Kevin piloted an airplane for
   a. 2,500 miles.   **b.** 5,000 miles.   **c.** 25,000 miles.

3. John Kevin began taking flying lessons when he was
   a. 9 years old.   **b.** 10 years old.   **c.** 11 years old.

4. It is against the law for anyone under 16 to
   a. fly an airplane.   **b.** fly an airplane alone.   **c.** fly an airplane with an adult pilot on board.

5. In 1989, John Kevin wants to
   a. become an astronaut.   **b.** go to the moon.   **c.** fly around the world.

Inferential Thinking

Circle the letter of the choice that best completes each item below.

1. You can conclude that a Cessna 210 is a kind of
   a. car.
   b. airplane.
   c. airport.

2. John Kevin cannot pilot a plane alone because
   a. he is not a good pilot.
   b. he gets frightened.
   c. he is under 16.

3. Which statement is a *fact*?
   a. Flying a plane is easy.
   b. Flying a plane is hard.
   c. John Kevin flew 2,500 miles.

4. Another good title for this selection is
   a. A Very Young Pilot.
   b. Flying Lessons.
   c. Flying to the Moon.

Critical Thinking

1. Do you think an 11-year-old should be allowed to fly an airplane? Give reasons for your answer.

   _____

2. Do you think it should be against the law for anyone under 16 to fly solo? Give reasons for your answer.

   _____

Vocabulary Development

Understanding Synonyms

Synonyms are two words that have similar meanings. In the reading selection, you read the words *alone* and *solo*. *Alone* and *solo* are synonyms.

Read each sentence below. Then circle the letter of the choice that is similar in meaning to the word printed in *italics*.

1. John Kevin says that flying a plane is *easy*.
   A synonym for *easy* is
   a. hard.   **b.** simple   **c.** wonderful.

2. He went on a long *trip* across the country.
   A synonym for *trip* is
   a. journey.   **b.** airplane.   **c.** way.

3. John Kevin's flying *instructor* went with him.
   A synonym for *instructor* is
   a. pilot.   **b.** follower.   **c.** teacher.

4. Mike Fields was with John Kevin in case there were any *problems*.
   A synonym for *problem* is
   a. solution.   **b.** answer.   **c.** trouble.

5. John Kevin was able to *pilot* the plane all the way by himself.
   A synonym for *pilot* is
   a. fly.   **b.** talk.   **c.** understand.

Test Taking

Read the following passage. Then complete the items below by filling in the correct choices in the answer grid.

John Kevin Hill made six stops on his flight from Los Angeles, California, to Washington, D.C. First, he landed in Cedar City, Utah. His next stops were Denver, Colorado, and Loveland, Colorado. Then, he went to Kansas City, Kansas, and St. Louis, Missouri. Cincinnati, Ohio, was his last stop before Washington. John Kevin landed at National Airport in Washington, D.C., on July 1, 1987. The next day he was greeted by Washington's most famous citizen, President Ronald Reagan.

1. John Kevin's first stop was in
  a. Cedar City, Utah.
  b. Kansas City, Kansas.
  c. Washington, D.C.

2. After John Kevin stopped in St. Louis, Missouri, he went to
  a. Denver, Colorado.
  b. Cedar City, Utah.
  c. Cincinnati, Ohio.

2. President Reagan greeted John Kevin in
  a. Los Angeles, California.
  b. Washington, D.C.
  c. Loveland, Colorado.

	a	b	c		a	b	c		a	b	c
1.	△	△	△	**2.**	△	△	△	**3.**	△	△	△

Applying Your Skills

Read the clues below, and fill in the correct words in the crossword puzzle. All of the answers are in the story, "Cross-Country Flyer."

Across
4. system for operating an airplane
5. what John Kevin wants to become when he grows up
6. famous person John Kevin met

Down
1. alone
2. where John Kevin's plane ended up
3. person who operates an airplane

INCA

The Inca Empire stretched from what is now Ecuador to what is now Chile. It included Peru and parts of Bolivia and Argentina. The Inca Empire reached its peak in the 15th and early 16th centuries.

- What do you know about the Incas?
- What happened to put an end to their mighty empire?

The land of the Incas stretched over 2,500 miles. The Incas had a very strong government that ran the empire. One man was the ruler. It was believed that his power came from the Sun God. People obeyed the ruler because they believed in the Sun God.

They also obeyed because the government took care of all the Inca people. The Incas were farmers. Each family was granted land by the government to farm. In return, the people had to give crops and service to the government. The Incas did not use money. There was enough of everything for everybody. Nobody was hungry. The government stored the food it received from the farmers. If crops were bad one year, the government gave everyone the food it had stored away.

The Incas loved beauty. They made wonderful stone buildings. They made cloth and pottery and worked with gold and silver. The Inca Empire was known as the land of gold.

The Incas called gold "the sweat of the sun." They loved gold because it was beautiful. Its value was not important to them because the Incas did not use money. They did not need to buy anything.

Yet, it was gold that caused the Inca Empire to come to an end. Spanish explorers had heard about the Incas' gold and wanted it for themselves. The Spaniards had horses, cannons, and rifles. They killed the Inca ruler and destroyed the mighty empire.

empire (EM pyr)   a large area of land ruled by one person or one country
centuries (SEN chur eez)   periods of one hundred years
service (SUR vis)   useful work
stored (STORD)   put away for future use
pottery (POT ur ee)   objects made from soft clay and hardened by heat

Direct Recall

Circle the letter of the choice that best completes each sentence.

1. The land of the Incas stretched over
   a. 2,500 miles.   **b.** 3,000 miles.   **c.** 3,500 miles.

2. The Inca Empire was ruled by
   a. one man.   **b.** a god.   **c.** a group of people.

3. The Inca people
   a. bought food with money.   **b.** did not use money.   **c.** did not have enough to eat.

4. The "sweat of the sun" was the Incas' name for
   a. money.   **b.** silver.   **c.** gold.

5. The Inca Empire was destroyed by
   a. French explorers.   **b.** Spanish explorers.   **c.** American explorers.

Inferential Thinking

Circle the letter of the choice that best completes each item below.

1. Which statement is *not* true?
   a. The Incas loved gold.
   b. The Spaniards loved gold.
   c. The Incas did not love gold.

2. You can conclude that the Incas had
   a. a lot of gold.
   b. a little gold.
   c. no gold.

3. The Spaniards destroyed the Inca Empire because they
   a. did not like the Incas.
   b. were greedy.
   c. did not have any money.

4. Which statement is an opinion?
   a. The Incas did not use money.
   b. The Spaniards killed the Inca ruler.
   c. The Spanish explorers were cruel.

Critical Thinking

1. What do you think about a society that does not use money?

_____

2. What was different about the Incas' love of gold and the Spanish explorers' love of gold?

_____

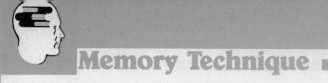

Using Questions to Remember Facts

There are many ways you can help yourself remember information when you read. One way is to ask yourself questions.

Read each question below. Then reread "Inca." Look for the answers to the questions as you read. Then write the answers in the spaces below. Use your own words.

1. What kind of government did the Incas have?

_____

2. Why did the Incas obey their ruler?

_____

3. What kinds of work did the Incas do?

_____

4. Why was nobody hungry in the Inca Empire?

_____

5. How did gold cause the Inca Empire to come to an end?

_____

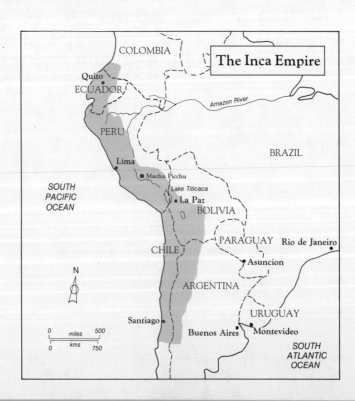

Test Taking

Read the following passage. Then complete the items below by filling in the correct choices in the answer grid.

The Spanish explorers captured the ruler of the Inca Empire, Atahualpa. Atahualpa knew that the Spaniards loved riches. He offered them enough gold and silver to fill a room as high as his hand could reach if they would set him free. The Spaniards accepted the offer. For two months, people from all over the empire brought gold and silver to the palace. The Spaniards took the gold and silver, but they killed Atahualpa anyway.

1. Atahualpa was
   a. a Spanish explorer.
   b. an Inca explorer.
   c. the ruler of the Incas.

2. Atahualpa offered to fill a room with gold and silver in exhange for
   a. his freedom.
   b. the Spaniards leaving his land.
   c. horses and guns.

3. Which word best describes what the Spaniards did?
   a. fair
   b. unfair
   c. honest

	a	b	c		a	b	c		a	b	c
1.	△	△	△	2.	△	△	△	3.	△	△	△

Applying Your Skills

Unscramble the letters in the words below. Each one is the name of a present-day country in South America where the Incas lived long ago.

1. ERUP   _____

2. EHLIC   _____

3. ABLIOVI   _____

4. DAREUCO   _____

5. GRENATANI _____

LAURA INGALLS WILDER

You may have read or heard of the *Little House* books by Laura Ingalls Wilder.
- Did you know that they are true stories?
- Did you know that they tell the story of the author's life?

Laura Ingalls Wilder was born in Pepin, Wisconsin, in 1867. She spent her childhood as a member of a pioneer family that was constantly moving westward. She moved with her family to Kansas, to Minnesota, and, finally, to the Dakota Territory.

Life was not easy for Laura's family. They had to build their own houses, make their own clothes, and grow or hunt their own food. They had to deal with failed crops, terrible weather, and even an invasion of grasshoppers. But, in spite of their problems, they had a lot of love, a lot of happiness, and a lot of fun.

One day in 1930, when Laura was 63 years old, she was thinking about her childhood and how different life was then. Laura wondered if people would remember what life was like for the pioneers. She even wondered if her own daughter would remember the stories she had heard.

Laura decided to write a book about her childhood. She would give it to her daughter Rose. Rose was a writer in New York City. As a child, Rose had always loved to hear stories about her mother's life as a pioneer.

Of course, Rose loved her mother's book. But she thought it was too good to keep for herself. Rose showed the book to an editor. *Little House in the Big Woods* was published in 1932. It was the first of nine *Little House* books. The books have been read and loved by people of all ages all over the world.

pioneer (py uh NEER) one of the first people to settle a region; a person who leads the way
crops (KROPS) plants grown to be used
invasion (in VAY zhun) an attack
editor (ED uh tur) a person who gets books ready to be published
published (PUB lisht) printed and offered for sale

Direct Recall

Circle the letter of the choice that best completes each sentence.

1. Laura Ingalls Wilder was born in
   a. Kansas. b. Minnesota. c. Wisconsin.

2. Laura's family kept moving
   a. east. b. west. c. south.

3. The Ingalls family had to deal with an invasion of
   a. soldiers. b. mosquitoes. c. grasshoppers.

4. Laura decided to write her first book in
   a. 1867. b. 1930. c. 1932.

5. Laura wrote *Little House in the Big Woods*
   a. for her daughter Rose. b. for herself. c. in order to get it published.

Inferential Thinking

Circle the letter of the choice that best completes each item below.

1. Which words best describe Laura's childhood?
   a. easy but happy
   b. hard but happy
   c. hard and unhappy

2. Weather would be important to the Ingalls family because
   a. they had to grow their own food.
   b. they liked to do things outside.
   c. they had no house.

3. The grasshoppers probably
   a. attacked the family.
   b. destroyed the Ingalls' house.
   c. ruined the Ingalls' crops.

4. How do you think Laura felt when she heard that her book was going to be published?
   a. surprised
   b. angry
   c. sad

Critical Thinking

1. In what ways do you think Laura Ingalls Wilder's childhood was different from yours?

2. Do you think it is important to have written records of the past? Give reasons for your answer.

Vocabulary Development

Using Context Clues

Read the following paragraph. Try to decide which word in the box fits each blank. Use the words before and after each blank to help you. Then reread the paragraph, and fill in the blanks correctly. Each word may be used only once. Make sure the word makes sense in the sentence and in the paragraph.

author	reason	refers	except	character

All of Laura Ingalls Wilder's books _____ *Farmer Boy*

are about her life. However, she never _____ to herself as

"I." The main _____ in the books is always called Laura.

The _____ never writes "*I* went west in a covered wagon."

She would say, "*Laura* went west in a covered wagon." The _____ Laura Ingalls Wilder decided to write that way was that she thought it made her books seem more like stories.

Test Taking

Read the following passage. Then complete the items below by filling in the correct choices in the answer grid.

Laura Ingalls Wilder did not plan to write another book after *Little House in the Big Woods*. But children kept writing to her, asking her for more stories. Laura didn't think of herself as a writer. She was very surprised by all the attention she received. Then, she decided to write about her husband Almanzo's childhood. She called the new book *Farmer Boy*. After *Farmer Boy* was published, Laura received even more letters. Everybody wanted to know what happened to Laura and what happened to Almanzo. It was then that Laura decided to write their whole story.

1. Which statement is correct?
   a. Laura always planned to write a lot of books.
   b. Laura always planned to write two books.
   c. Laura planned to write only one book.

2. Laura's second book was
   a. *Little House in the Big Woods*.
   b. *Little House on the Prairie*.
   c. *Farmer Boy*.

3. The second was about
   a. Laura's childhood.
   b. Almanzo's childhood.
   c. Laura and Almanzo's life together.

	a	b	c		a	b	c		a	b	c
1.	△	△	△	**2.**	△	△	△	**3.**	△	△	△

Applying Your Skills

Suppose you were the publisher of *Little House in the Big Woods*. Write an ad for the book.

13

UNCLE TOM'S CABIN

A book can be something that entertains you. It can also be something that teaches you.
- How can a book also influence history?
- What did *Uncle Tom's Cabin* have to do with the Civil War?

It was something that had never happened before. A white person wrote a book in which the hero was black and the villain was white.

The year was 1852. The book was *Uncle Tom's Cabin*. Harriet Beecher Stowe was the author. Mrs. Stowe was an abolitionist. She believed that slavery was wrong and must be stopped.

The hero of her book was a kind old slave named Uncle Tom. The villain was the cruel Simon Legree. The book showed the evils of slavery. Thousands of people read *Uncle Tom's Cabin*.

Many northerners praised Mrs. Stowe. They felt that she had described slavery as it really was. Many southerners were angered by Mrs. Stowe. They said she had no right to criticize the South. They felt that she didn't know anything about slavery.

Uncle Tom's Cabin became a call to action. For people in the North, it was a call to put an end to slavery. For people in the South, it was a call to protect their way of life.

Many people think that *Uncle Tom's Cabin* helped bring on the Civil War. Abraham Lincoln once called Harriet Beecher Stowe "the little lady who started this big war." He was exaggerating, of course, but there was some truth to what he said.

influence (IN floo uns) have an effect on; change
hero (HEER oh) the main good character in a story
villain (VIL un) a wicked person in a story
abolitionist (ab uh LISH uh nist) a person who favored ending slavery
exaggerating (eg ZAJ uh rayt ing) making something seem more than it is

Direct Recall

Circle the letter of the choice that best completes each sentence.

1. The author of *Uncle Tom's Cabin* was
   a. Uncle Tom.   **b.** Simon Legree.   **c.** Harriet Beecher Stowe.

2. The hero of the book was
   a. Uncle Tom.   **b.** Simon Legree.   **c.** Harriet Beecher Stowe.

3. The villain of the book was
   a. Uncle Tom.   **b.** Simon Legree.   **c.** Harriet Beecher Stowe

4. *Uncle Tom's Cabin* angered many southerners because they felt that
   a. Mrs. Stowe hated the South.   **b.** Mrs. Stowe loved the North.
   c. Mrs. Stowe didn't know anything about slavery.

5. Many people think the book helped bring on
   a. the American Revolution.   **b.** the Civil War.   **c.** World War I.

Inferential Thinking

Circle the letter of the choice that best completes each item below.

1. This selection is mainly about
   a. Harriet Beecher Stowe's life.
   b. the book *Uncle Tom's Cabin*.
   c. the Civil War.

2. How do you think the idea of slavery made
   Harriet Beecher Stowe feel?
   a. happy
   b. uninterested
   c. angry

3. You can conclude that Harriet Beecher
   Stowe
   a. lived in the North.
   b. lived in the South.
   c. lived in the West.

4. You can conclude that Abraham Lincoln
   thought *Uncle Tom's Cabin*
   a. was the only cause of the Civil War.
   b. helped bring on the Civil War.
   c. had nothing to do with the Civil War.

Critical Thinking

1. Why do you think Harriet Beecher Stowe wrote *Uncle Tom's Cabin*?

_____

2. How do you think books can influence history?

_____

15

Creating a Memory Map

One way to remember information from a story is to make a memory map. A memory map is an outline of the details in a story. Some of the details in a story may answer the questions *who, what, when,* and *why?*

Reread *Uncle Tom's Cabin.* Then fill in the memory map below.

Who wrote *Uncle Tom's Cabin?*

_____

What was *Uncle Tom's Cabin?*

_____

When was *Uncle Tom's Cabin* published?

_____

Why was *Uncle Tom's Cabin* important?

_____

_____

Test Taking

Read the following passage. Then answer the questions by filling in the correct choices in the answer grid.

> The publisher of *Uncle Tom's Cabin* was afraid that the book wouldn't sell. Harriet Beecher Stowe just hoped enough copies would be sold to earn her money to buy a silk dress. More than 300,000 copies of the book were sold in its first year in the United States. Another 150,000 copies were sold in England. The book was reprinted over and over again. It was translated into other languages and sold all over the world. It was the most talked about book of its time.

1. The publisher of *Uncle Tom's Cabin* thought the book would
   a. be a best seller.
   b. be very popular.
   c. not sell.

2. You can conclude that Harriet Beecher Stowe
   a. did not get her silk dress.
   b. did get her silk dress.
   c. did not want a silk dress.

3. How many copies of *Uncle Tom's Cabin* were sold in its first year in the United States?
   a. 150,000
   b. more than 300,000
   c. 450,000

	a b c		a b c		a b c
1.	△ △ △	2.	△ △ △	3.	△ △ △

Applying Your Skills

Use each clue to fill in the blanks below. All the words in the puzzle are words you read in the book *Uncle Tom's Cabin*. When you finish, write the letters in the circles on the blanks at the bottom of the page. They will spell out a word that Harriet Beecher Stowe would use to describe slavery.

1. the main good character   _ ⃝ _ _

2. a wicked person in a story   ⃝ _ _ _ _ _ _

3. making something seem more than it is   _ _ _ _ _ _ _ _ ⃝ _ _

4. a person who favored ending slavery   _ _ _ ⃝ _ _ _ _ _ _

$$\overline{} \ \overline{} \ \overline{} \ \overline{}$$
1 2 3 4

NARCISSUS

The ancient Greeks told stories about gods and goddesses. This myth tells the story of what happened to a boy who loved himself more than he loved other people.

- Do you know people who think they are better than everyone else?
- Do you like people like that? Why?

Once there was a boy named Narcissus. When he was born, his mother was told that her son would live a long life if he never saw himself.

Narcissus grew up happy and playful. He also grew up to be very beautiful. All the girls who saw him fell in love with him and wanted to kiss him. But he wanted nothing of love. He thought it was nonsense. Narsissus did not love anybody.

One of the girls who loved him was named Echo. She could only repeat what other people said to her.

"I don't want you to kiss me," Narcissus said to Echo angrily.

"Kiss me. Kiss me," repeated Echo hopefully.

Narcissus walked away. Echo ran off forever to hide her sorrow in the lonely caves of the world. She still lives in places like that. Sometimes, if you call to her, she will answer you.

The Goddess of Love heard how Narcissus had hurt Echo's feelings. The goddess did not like people to be so careless about love. Thus, to punish Narcissus, she made him fall in love with himself.

One day, as Narcissus bent down beside a pool of water to take a drink, he saw his own reflection for the first time. Instantly, he was in love with the beautiful boy he saw in the water.

"I want to be with you forever," Narcissus said to his reflection. He never left that spot and soon died. After his death, a flower grew in the place where he had died. That flower is called the narcissus.

---

nonsense (NON sens) foolish behavior, actions, or ideas
angrily (AN grih lee) in a way that shows anger
reflection (rih FLEK shun) an image given back to one, as from a mirror
narcissus (nar SIS us) the name of a white or yellow flower

Direct Recall

Circle the letter of the choice that best completes each sentence.

1. Narcissus' mother was told her son would live a long life if he
   a. worked hard.   **b.** never saw himself.   **c.** looked at his reflection.

2. All the girls
   a. fell in love with Narcissus.   **b.** did not like Narcissus.   **c.** repeated what other people said.

3. Echo ran away and hid in
   a. the woods.   **b.** an old house.   **c.** the caves of the world.

4. The Goddess of Love made Narcissus fall in love with
   a. her.   **b.** himself.   **c.** Echo.

5. "I want to be with you forever," Narcissus said to
   a. the Goddess of Love.   **b.** Echo.   **c.** his reflection.

Inferential Thinking

Circle the letter of the choice that best completes each item below.

1. The warning given to Narcissus' mother
   a. came true.
   b. did not come true.
   c. was foolish.

2. How did the Goddess of Love feel when she heard about Narcissus?
   a. happy
   b. angry
   c. amused

3. Narcissus fell in love when he saw
   a. Echo.
   b. the Goddess of Love.
   c. his reflection.

4. The narcissus is probably
   a. an ugly flower.
   b. a plain flower.
   c. a pretty flower.

Critical Thinking

1. Why do you think the Goddess of Love punished Narcissus the way she did?

   _____

2. Do you think the Goddess of Love's punishment for Narcissus was fair? Give reasons for your answer.

   _____

Vocabulary Development

Learning Word Histories

Words have histories. Many words come from other languages. You can learn about a word's history, or *etymology*, by looking in a dictionary.

In the reading selection, you read about Narcissus and Echo. Look at the two dictionary entries below.

narcissism (NAR suh siz um)   too much love for oneself (this word comes from an ancient Greek word)

echo (EK oh)   the repeating of a sound (this word comes from an ancient Greek word)

Look at each word in the column on the left. Match the word with its definition and etymology.

1. moose   type of dance (French)
2. judo   stringed musical instrument (African)
3. easel   very large North American animal (Native American)
4. banjo   method of self-defense (Japanese)
5. ballet   frame that holds the canvas on which an artist paints (Dutch)

Test Taking

Read the following passage. Then answer the questions by filling in the correct choices in the answer grid.

People have always tried to understand the mysteries of nature. Today, we have science to help us. But years ago, people told stories about powerful gods and goddesses to explain things that they could not understand. One myth explains the change of seasons. Another tells about the origin of thunder. The myth you have just read tells how a flower came to be named the narcissus.

1. People in ancient times told stories about gods and goddesses to explain
   a. things they knew about.
   b. things they did not understand.
   c. why there were gods.

2. You can conclude that the ancient Greeks
   a. believed in one god.
   b. did not believe in god.
   c. believed in many gods.

3. You can conclude that the word *origin* means
   a. beginning.
   b. word.
   c. color.

	a	b	c		a	b	c		a	b	c
1.	△	△	△	2.	△	△	△	3.	△	△	△

Applying Your Skills

Make up your own myth explaining something in nature. Write it in the space below. Use a separate sheet of paper if you need more space.

_____

_____

_____

_____

_____

_____

_____

_____

_____

_____

LEAP YEAR

There are generally 365 days in a year. But this is not always true.
- What is a leap year?
- Why are leap years needed?

A year is the length of time it takes the earth to revolve around the sun. A day is the length of time it takes the earth to turn on its axis. A year is 365 days, 5 hours, 48 minutes, and 46 seconds long. Since a day has 24 hours, that means a year is almost 365.25 days long.

There is a problem putting 365.25 days on a calendar. One year, days would start at midnight. The next year, they would start at 6:00 in the morning. The following year, days would start at noon. The year after that, they would start at 6:00 at night.

To avoid this confusion, most years on the calendar have 365 days. Every four years, though, we have what is called a leap year, a year with 366 days. The day that is added is Feburary 29.

However, since a year is really a little less than 365.25 days long, there is still a problem. Adding an extra day every four years would make the average year 11 minutes and 14 seconds too long. To take care of this problem, we don't add an extra day in most century years (1700, 1800, 1900). But even this doesn't completely solve the problem. So we do add an extra day in century years that can be evenly divided by 4 (1200, 1600, 2000).

You'd think that would take care of everything, but it doesn't. In the year 4000, a day will have to be dropped. Do you think people at that time will worry about it?

revolve (rih VOLV)   move around in an orbit
axis (AK sis)   a real or imaginary line around which something, such as the earth, turns or seems to turn
avoid (uh VOID)   stay away from
confusion (kun FYOO zhun)   being mixed up or bewildered

Direct Recall

Circle the letter of the choice that best completes each sentence.

1. A year is
   a. exactly 365 days long.   b. 365 days, 5 hours, 48 minutes, and 46 seconds long.
   c. 366 days, 5 hours, 48 minutes, and 46 seconds long.

2. Most years on the calendar have
   a. 365 days.   b. 365.25 days.   c. 366 days.

3. Every four years we
   a. add an extra day to the calendar.   b. drop a day from the calendar.
   c. don't change the calendar.

4. In most century years, we
   a. add an extra day to the calendar.   b. add two extra days to the calendar.
   c. don't add an extra day to the calendar.

5. A day will have to be dropped from the calendar in the year
   a. 4000.   b. 5000.   c. 6000.

Inferential Thinking

Circle the letter of the choice that best completes each item below.

1. What would be the problem with having 365.25 days on the calendar?
   a. Each year, days would start at a different time of day.
   b. There would be no problem.
   c. There would be no February 29.

2. Leap year usually takes place
   a. every four years.
   b. every six years.
   c. every 100 years.

3. February 29 appears on the calendar
   a. every year
   b. only in leap years.
   c. every five years.

4. Which statement is *not* true?
   a. A day has 24 hours.
   b. A year is the time it takes the earth to go around the sun.
   c. Every year is the same on the calendar.

Critical Thinking

1. How do you think scientists know how long a year is?

   _____

2. Why is it important to have the length of the calendar year be the same as the length of time it takes the earth to revolve around the sun?

   _____

Memory Technique

Using Key Words

Writing down key words is a good way to remember information. *Key words* are important words or groups of words that will remind you of what you have read. Look for key words when you read for information.

The following key words are from the selection "Leap Year." In your own words, tell what the key words make you remember from the reading. Look back at the reading selection if you need help.

1. year _____

2. day _____

3. leap year _____

4. February 29 _____

5. century years _____

Test Taking

Look at the dictionary entry. Then complete the items below by filling in the correct choices in the answer grid.

> **calendar** (KAL un dur)   a table showing the days, weeks, and months of the year

1. How many syllables does the word *calendar* have?
   a. two
   b. three
   c. four

2. The accent is on the _____ syllable.
   a. first
   b. second
   c. third

3. What form of speech is the word *calendar*?
   a. noun
   b. verb
   c. adjective

	a b c		a b c		a b c
1.	△ △ △	2.	△ △ △	3.	△ △ △

Applying Your Skills

A year is a leap year if you can divide it by 4. The year 1980 was a leap year. The year 1984 was a leap year. Fill in the chart below. You must figure out whether each of the years in the chart is a leap year or not.

	Year	Leap Year? (yes or no)
1. the year you were born		
2. this year		
3. next year		
4. last year		
5. the year you will graduate from high school		

DAEDALUS 88

This year, for the first time in history, a man successfully flew through the air by using his legs and feet. It happened off the coast of Greece, in the same place where a character in an ancient Greek story also flew through the air. The difference was that he used his arms.

- Have you ever dreamed you could fly?
- If you could fly by yourself, where would you go?

Recently, a team of scientists built a new kind of airplane. They took it to Greece. Greece is an ancient country that has hundreds of beautiful islands. The plane flew from one island to another.

One of the strangest things about this new airplane is that it is built like a bicycle. In fact, only one person can ride in it at a time. That's right! And that person has to use both legs and feet to pedal, the same as on a bike.

How can just one person propel an airplane? You can find the answer by looking at the picture. See how long the wings are? They are more than 100 feet long, almost as long as four telephone poles put together. These long wings help lift the plane into the air with ease.

The scientists who built the plane picked a champion bicycle racer to pedal it. He traveled 74 miles in less than four hours. Even though the aircraft didn't go very fast, it was able to fly pretty high. It flew more than 15 feet above the sea. Think how beautiful the pink and silver plane must have looked in the morning sun.

The scientists called their flying machine the *Daedalus 88*. They named it after a man in an ancient Greek legend. In the legend, Daedalus made wings for himself and his son Icarus from bird feathers and wax, which they attached to their arms. With their wings, they flew away from the Greek island of Crete.

In 1988, the flying machine *Daedalus* flew away from the same island.

successfully (suk SES fuh lee)   with a good result
ancient (AYN shunt)   from long ago
strangest (STRAYNJ ust)   most different or peculiar; oddest
champion (CHAM pee un)   the best
legend (LEJ und)   ancient story

Direct Recall

Circle the letter of the choice that best completes each sentence.

1. The new kind of airplane flew from one island to
   a. the mountains.   **b.** a city.   **c.** another island.

2. The plane is built like a
   a. boat.   **b.** bicycle.   **c.** rocket.

3. The number of people that can ride in the plane at the same time is
   a. one.   **b.** five.   **c.** two.

4. The length of the wings is
   a. six feet.   **b.** 100 feet.   **c.** more than 100 feet.

5. The one who pedaled the plane was a
   a. scientist.   **b.** champion swimmer.   **c.** champion bicycle racer.

Inferential Thinking

Circle the letter of the choice that best completes each item below.

1. The new airplane was able to fly because
   a. the sun was shining.
   b. the driver pedaled very fast.
   c. it was pink and silver.

2. You can conclude that Greece is
   a. by the sea.
   b. close to your home.
   c. not a real place.

3. Another good title for this story would be
   a. "Fly Like a Bird."
   b. "The Champion."
   c. "A Legend Comes to Life."

4. The scientists probably tested the plane to
   a. make a different kind of bicycle.
   b. take a trip to Greece.
   c. discover new ways to fly.

Critical Thinking

1. Why do you think the scientists chose a champion bicycle racer to fly their new plane?

_____

2. Do you think it is possible for a person to fly with wings made from feathers and wax? Why or why not?

_____

Vocabulary Development

Using Context Clues

Read each sentence below. Then fill in the blank with the word that fits best in the sentence.

1. The flight of *Daedalus 88* was _____ completed.

   successfully   strangest

2. The long wings helped _____ the plane into the air.

   raise   fall

3. There was a _____ about a man named Daedalus.

   legend   scientist

4. The story came from long ago. It is very _____

   ancient   champion

5. It was the _____ plane people had ever seen.

   champion   strangest

6. They chose a _____ bicycle racer because he had strong legs.

   champion   legend

Test Taking

Read the following passage. Then complete the items below by filling in the correct choices in the answer grid.

Throughout history, people have wanted to fly. Stories from long ago tell of men flying with wings or riding in the air on magic carpets. Before there were airplanes, some people used large balloons filled with hot air to take them high in the sky. The first airplane was built less than 100 years ago. Now, people fly every day all over the world. Rockets have taken people to the moon. Soon we may be able to fly far into space. Maybe you will have a chance to go during your lifetime.

1. This selection is mainly about
   a. different ways to fly.
   b. airplanes.
   c. space travel.

2. The first airplane was built
   a. before balloons.
   b. less than 100 years ago.
   c. to fly to the moon.

3. You can conclude from reading this that
   a. more people fly today than ever before.
   b. you will visit the moon.
   c. trains are better than planes.

	a	b	c		a	b	c		a	b	c
1.	△	△	△	2.	△	△	△	3.	△	△	△

Applying Your Skills

You are the owner of a plane that you can ride like a bicycle. Where would you like to go? List the places you would visit with this new way of getting around. Tell what you would do when you arrived at each place.

Places I Would Visit   **What I Would Do**

_____   _____

_____   _____

_____   _____

_____   _____

29

DOGS: THE FIRST FRIENDS

There are many different kinds of dogs. Try looking at all the dogs you can see as you walk down the street. Look at the differences in size, shape, and color. Did you know that all of these animals are related to one another? They all have the same ancestors.

- Why do dogs make such good pets?
- How do you think wild dogs became tame?

In the United States, almost half of all families have pets. Many of these pets are dogs. People choose dogs as pets because dogs are smart and loyal. In addition, dogs like people and try to please them. A dog can be a wonderful friend.

Of all the wild animals, dogs were the first to be friendly to people. Scientists believe that dogs began to be tamed about 12,000 years ago.

How do scientists know this? In certain places where people lived long ago, scientists uncovered bones of dogs together with the bones of those early people. It seemed to the scientists that the dogs must have lived with the people. The scientists conducted tests on the bones they had dug up to find out how old the bones were. They found out that the bones were very old indeed.

Since early times, dogs have been so useful to people that more and more different breeds of dog have been developed. For example, people developed hunting dogs with a strong sense of smell and keen eyesight. People developed fast dogs for racing, large dogs for protection, and pretty dogs to keep as pets.

There are many more breeds of dog than there are of other animals. While there are different breeds of cows and horses and cats, they are not as different from each other as dogs are. Today, there are more than four hundred breeds of dog.

related (rih LAYT id)   being of the same family or kind
ancestors (AN ses turs)   early animals from which later kinds have developed
scientist (SY un tist)   an expert in a science
breed (BREED)   a special kind of animal or plant

Direct Recall

Circle the letter of the choice that best completes each sentence.

1. In the United States, almost half of all families have
   a. dogs. **b.** pets. **c.** cats.

2. People began to tame dogs
   a. just now. **b.** in pioneer times. **c.** 12,000 years ago.

3. Scientists found bones of dogs together with those of
   a. buffalo. **b.** people. **c.** other animals.

4. There are so many different breeds of dog because
   a. they are so useful. **b.** they came from many different ancestors.
   c. they came from many parts of the world.

5. Hunting dogs were developed
   a. to be pets. **b.** with a strong sense of smell. **c.** to be friendly to people.

Inferential Thinking

Circle the letter of the choice that best completes each item below.

1. This story is mainly about
   a. how to train dogs.
   b. where dogs came from.
   c. how dogs need people.

2. Another good title for this story would be
   a. "A Friend with Four Legs."
   b. "Life with Early People."
   c. "How to Train a Dog."

3. Very strong dogs are useful
   a. as house pets.
   b. to pull things.
   c. to do circus tricks.

4. Hunting dogs need a keen sense of smell and good eyesight to
   a. find their way home.
   b. smell and sight their prey.
   c. recognize their owners.

Critical Thinking

1. What are some qualities that you would like your friends to have? Which of these qualities can a dog have?

_____

_____

2. Do you think that dogs are happier living in the country or living in the city? Give reasons for your answer.

_____

_____

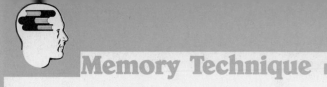

Completing a Time Line

One way to remember the order of important details is to make a time line. A time line shows the order in which things happen. This will help you to remember information.

Read the following sentences about animals. Write each animal's name on the time line in the correct place. The first one is done for you.

Scientists think that dogs were tamed about 12,000 years ago and sheep about 11,000 years ago. People began to keep wild goats about 9,000 years ago. Horses were tamed about 5,000 ago. Cats first became pets in Egypt about 4,000 years ago.

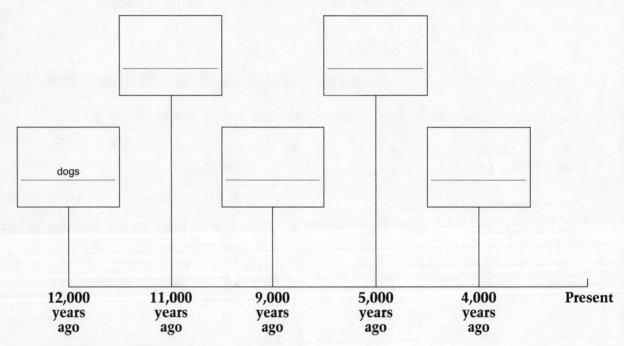

| 12,000 years ago | 11,000 years ago | 9,000 years ago | 5,000 years ago | 4,000 years ago | Present |

Study your time line. Then answer the following questions:

1. Which animals were tamed before sheep? _____

2. Which animals were tamed earlier, sheep or goats? _____

3. Which animals were the last to be tamed? _____

Test Taking

Read the following passage. Then complete the items below by filling in the correct choices in the answer grid.

Dogs are not the only animals that people tamed. People have other animal friends that work for them, feed and clothe them, and keep them company. Some animals are raised for food. Others are raised for what they can produce. All these animals had ancestors that were wild until people tamed them and bred them to be different.

1. This paragraph is mainly about
   a. animals that help people.
   b. animals that are good pets.
   c. how people get pets.

2. All tame animals
   a. like to do tricks.
   b. have ancestors that were wild.
   c. always stay indoors.

3. Animals are raised so that people can
   a. have things to eat and wear.
   b. train them to be wild.
   c. grow fruits and vegetables.

	a	b	c		a	b	c		a	b	c
1.	△	△	△	2.	△	△	△	3.	△	△	△

Applying Your Skills

Look at the cartoon below. What does it tell you about the way dogs feel? Do you think the cartoon is right?

_____

_____

_____

_____

_____

_____

_____

THE QUIETEST BOY IN CLASS

School was unpleasant for Thor Heyerdahl (Tor HAY-ur-dol). He was not only the youngest boy in his class but he was also the smallest. He was shy. He hated sports. Worst of all, he was afraid of the water.

- Are you afraid of the water? If you are, do you know why?
- Can you guess what Thor became when he grew up?

Thor Heyerdahl was the quietest and shyest boy in his class. When the other children played games, he just watched them. In sports, he was hopeless. He could not learn to swim.

Thor liked living things. He gathered insects and tiny water animals. He liked adventures, too. Sometimes he wrote stories and drew pictures. Most of his stories were about children who sailed to faraway islands.

or grew up, he had adventures of his own. He became a scientist. He traveled to many exciting places.

Thor visited many islands in the South Pacific. He noticed that certain people on the islands did not look the same as other islanders. These people had pale skin and different features. Thor thought about this strange fact. He finally decided that these people had come from faraway Peru a long time ago. He thought they must have come across the ocean.

The experts thought that Thor was crazy. "Boats made of logs could not come so far," they said. The experts thought that the people would have drowned on the trip.

Thor was sure the experts were wrong. He studied the kind of boats people used long ago. Then, he built a boat exactly like them. He named his boat *Kon-Tiki*.

Thor sailed the *Kon-Tiki* from South America all the way to an island near Tahiti. The trip was 4,000 miles long. It took more than three months. Thor Heyerdahl proved that people on log rafts could have sailed across the ocean long ago. He proved this by doing it himself.

adventures (ud VEN churz)   unusual, exciting, or dangerous experiences
islanders (EYE lund urz)   people living on islands
Peru (puh ROO)   a country on the western coast of South America
features (FEE churz)   parts of the faces, such as the eyes, the nose, and the mouth
experts (EK spurts)   people who have much special knowledge and experience
Tahiti (Tuh HEET ee)   an island in the South Pacific

Direct Recall

Circle the letter of the choice that best completes each sentence.

1. As a child, Thor was interested in
   a. living things.   b. motorbikes.   c. all sports.

2. He was afraid of
   a. animals.   b. school.   c. the water.

3. When Thor grew up, he became a
   a. famous athlete.   b. scientist.   c. a soldier.

4. Experts thought that log boats could not
   a. float.   b. travel so far.   c. be made.

5. Thor Heyerdahl named his boat
   a. *Peru.*   b. *Kon-Tiki.*   c. *Tahiti.*

Inferential Thinking

Circle the letter of the choice that best completes each item below.

1. You can tell that Thor Heyerdahl
   a. thought he was right.
   b. was not very smart.
   c. liked building boats.

2. Thor probably did not learn to swim because he
   a. was not very strong.
   b. was afraid of the water.
   c. was too small.

3. Thor Heyerdahl sailed across the ocean because he
   a. loved the sea.
   b. wanted to show it could be done.
   c. was a sailor.

4. From reading the story, you can tell that experts
   a. are always right.
   b. can sometimes be wrong.
   c. like the ocean.

Critical Thinking

1. Many people admire Thor Heyerdahl. Do you admire him? Give reasons for your answers.

_____

_____

_____

2. What makes a person a hero?

_____

_____

_____

Vocabulary Development

Using the suffix -less

The reading selection tells you that Thor Heyerdahl was hopeless in sports. The suffix- *less* means without. *Hopeless* means "without hope."

Add the suffix- *less* to make new words. Then give the meaning of the new words.

	New word	**Meaning**
1. air	_____	_____
2. child	_____	_____
3. worth	_____	_____
4. tooth	_____	_____
5. sleep	_____	_____

Now write a sentence using each of the new words you made. Be sure that each sentence shows that you understand what the word means.

1. _____

2. _____

3. _____

4. _____

5. _____

Test Taking

Read the following paragraph. Then answer the questions below. Put your answers in the grid.

Thor and his friends started to build the raft. First, they picked nine of the biggest logs they could find. They tied the logs together with rope. They did not use any nails because nails were not used long ago. Then, the men cut some smaller logs. They tied them crosswise on top to make the raft stronger. They made a little cabin on the deck. This was to sleep in. Last, they made a big sail. They named their boat *Kon-Tiki*.

1. The *Kon-Tiki* was made of
  a. steel.
  b. logs.
  c. plastic.

2. The raft was held together by
  a. nails.
  b. rope.
  c. glue.

3. The thing that made the *Kon-Tiki* move was
  a. a motor.
  b. a paddle wheel.
  c. the wind.

	a	b	c		a	b	c		a	b	c
1.	△	△	△	**2.**	△	△	△	**3.**	△	△	△

Applying Your Skills

Look at the map below. The *Kon-Tiki* sailed from the coast of Peru. It sailed more than 4,000 miles. It landed on a small island. With your pencil, draw the raft's trip. Then answer the questions below.

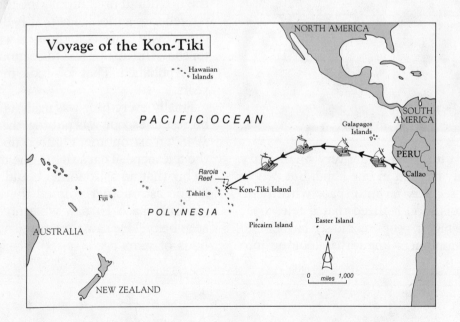

Take this trip in your mind. Would you be afraid? What do you think some of the dangers might be?

THE BIG EYE IN THE SKY

Have you ever seen a picture of your grandparents when they were young? If you have, you have looked back in time. Using telescopes is another way of looking back in time.
- Would you like to look into the future?
- Do you think telescopes are easy to make?

The first telescopes were very small. They could easily be held in one hand. But people could not see very far into space with them. Astronomers soon realized that if telescopes were made bigger, people could see farther into space. Astronomers knew that looking into space is like looking back in time. The stars seen through telescopes are very old. The stars tell a lot about the universe.

Astronomers were eager to learn more about the universe. So they started making bigger and bigger telescopes to see the stars. The bigger the telescopes became, the harder it was to make them.

In 1928, work began on the world's biggest telescope. It was to be twice as big as any one then in existence. Every step in its construction had to be planned and carried out very, very carefully. If everything was not exactly right, the telescope would not work. The most important part of the telescope was the mirror, which gathers light from the stars. In 1934, the hot liquid used in making the mirror was poured into a mold. Then, it had to be cooled very slowly. This took almost a whole year. After that, the mirror had to be ground and carefully polished. That job took more than ten years.

Finally, everything was ready, and the world's biggest telescope was put together. On June 3, 1948, an astronomer climbed up and got into the telescope. That's right. The telescope was so big that an astronomer could sit *inside* it.

The astronomer pointed the telescope far out into space. He saw what no one had ever seen before! He saw the universe as it was billions of years ago.

astronomers (uh STRAHN uh murz)   scientists who study the stars
universe (YOO nuh vurs)   the whole world
liquid (LIK wid)   a substance that flows freely, like water
billion (BIL yun)   a thousand million; 1,000,000,000
observatory (ub ZER vuh tawr ee)   a building that houses telescopes

Direct Recall

Circle the letter of the choice that best completes each sentence.

1. When you look at the stars, you are
   a. looking back in time.   **b.** looking forward in time.   **c.** seeing what's happening right now.

2. The first telescopes were
   a. small   **b.** large.   **c.** in-between.

3. The bigger the telescope,
   a. the less you can see.   **b.** the farther you can see.   **c.** the less difference it makes.

4. They started to plan the world's biggest telescope in
   a. 1982.   **b.** 1928.   **c.** 1892.

5. The astronomer sits
   a. on top of this telescope.   **b.** behind this telescope.   **c.** inside this telescope.

Inferential Thinking

Circle the letter of the choice that best completes each item below.

1. For an astronomer, a good telescope is
   a. very important.
   b. rather important.
   c. not important.

2. From the time they started till the time they finished, the construction of the telescope took
   a. 2 years.
   b. 20 years.
   c. 200 years.

3. You can conclude that making a big telescope takes a
   a. long time and is hard to do.
   b. short time and is easy to do.
   c. long time but is easy to do.

4. The bigger a telescope is, the
   a. less you can see in space.
   b. sooner the astronomer can go home.
   c. more information you can get by using it.

Critical Thinking

1. Do you think scientists should keep making bigger and bigger telescopes? Why?

_____

2. What good does it do to look at the stars?

_____

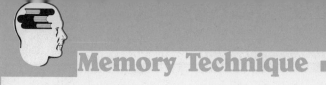

Memory Technique

Working with a Time Line

A good way to remember important details in a story is to make a time line. A time line shows the order in which things happened. This will help you remember the information.

Read the following paragraph. Then fill in the time line with the correct information.

In 1928, scientists decided to make the world's biggest telescope. It was very hard to do. The hardest part was to figure out how to make the mirror. In 1934, they started making the great mirror. The next year, they started to grind and polish it. This took many years to do. In 1945, they began to put the telescope together. In 1948, it was all finished.

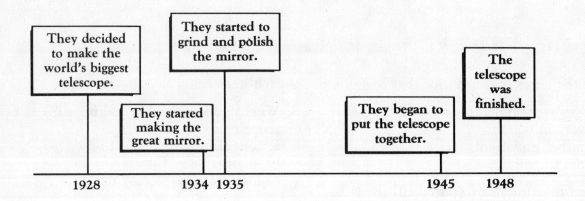

Answer the following questions, using the time line.

1. After they ground and polished the mirror, what did they do?

_____

2. When did they decide to make the big telescope?

_____

3. When was the telescope finished?

_____

40

Test Taking

Read the following passage. Then complete the items below by filling in the correct choices in the answer grid.

George Ellery Hale was a famous astronomer. The big telescope was named in his honor. The Hale Telescope is in an observatory on a mountain in Southern California. Observatories are built on mountains because the air is clearer there than anywhere else. It is most important for astronomers to see the stars as clearly as possible.

1. The Hale Telescope is named for
   a. Nathan Hale.
   b. General Ellery Hale.
   c. George Ellery Hale.

2. This passage is mainly about
   a. where observatories are located.
   b. George Ellery Hale.
   c. when the telescope was built.

3. Observatories are built on mountains because
   a. the air is clearer there.
   b. astronomers like to be close to the stars.
   c. there is less noise.

	a	b	c		a	b	c		a	b	c
1.	△	△	△	2.	△	△	△	3.	△	△	△

Applying Your Skills

You are an astronomer on a different planet. You are looking through your telescope to find out if there is life on Earth. You can see highways and buildings. List ten more things that might tell you there is life on Earth.

HOW DRUMS CAME TO BE

Long before stories were written down, they were told by "talking" drums. African drummers say that when the world was made, a drummer was the first person to appear on earth. Drums have been used for a long time. People use drums to tell what they feel.

● Why do you think there are drums?
● How do you think drums were invented?

Long ago, Sun looked down on his people on Earth. He saw that they were quiet and sad. Sun said, "I must do something for them." Sun sent for Coyote, who lived on Earth and knew how the people there felt.

"The people hear wonderful sounds all around them," Coyote told Sun. "They hear the water rushing down the mountains. They hear the wind blowing. They have these sounds inside them but no way to let the sounds out."

Sun said, "Go back to Earth. Find a way to call out the sounds from the people's hearts."

Coyote had a plan. He went to a hunting camp. He crept into the tepee of a young hunter and stole all the animal skins.

When the young hunter found that his skins had been stolen, he was very angry. Luckily, the hunting was good and the young man killed and skinned another large elk. He carried the skin to his tepee and flung it down. Later, he saw that the skin had landed too near the fire and its hair was burned off. He picked up the skin and threw it over a hollow stump. Then, he went hunting again and was gone for many days.

When the young man returned, it was time to leave the camp. The hunter began to collect his things. He tried to pull the skin off the stump. It was stuck and would not come off.

"Hurry up," called the rest of the people in the camp. The hunter pulled at the skin with all his strength. Still it would not come off. He was very angry at the skin. He picked up a club and hit it with all his might.

The skin gave out a great noise like thunder! The hunter was amazed. He beat the skin many times more. It was the sound of the first drum.

The people came back when they heard the drum. It seemed that the voice in the drum was speaking the feelings in their hearts. They began to dance and sing with joy.

coyote (ky OHT ee)   a small wolf
tepee (TEE pee)   a tent made of animal skins and shaped like a cone
elk (ELK)   a large deer
disgusted (dis GUST id)   feeling sick, as from a bad smell
amazed (uh MAYZD)   greatly surprised; astonished
buffaloes (BUF uh lohz)   wild oxen
plains (PLAYNZ)   large, flat expanses of land

Direct Recall

Circle the letter of the choice that best completes each sentence.

1. Sun saw that people were
   a. hungry.   b. sad.   c. angry.

2. Sun told Coyote to
   a. make a drum.   b. steal the skin.   c. go back to Earth.

3. Coyote had a
   a. drum.   b. plan.   c. promise.

4. The young hunter threw the fresh elk skin
   a. over a hollow stump.   b. on the ground.   c. in the air.

5. The elk skin would not come off because it was
   a. stuck.   b. unhappy.   c. too big.

Inferential Thinking

Circle the letter of the choice that best completes each item below.

1. You can tell that Coyote was
   a. clever.
   b. sad.
   c. angry.

2. Coyote stole the hunter's skins because he wanted
   a. furs for himself.
   b. the hunter to get a fresh skin.
   c. the tepee to be empty.

3. The hunter hit the skin with the club because he
   a. wanted to make music.
   b. was angry.
   c. was hungry.

4. You can tell that the hunter had a
   a. kind heart.
   b. hot temper.
   c. many friends.

Critical Thinking

1. Do you think Coyote needed a hunter with a quick temper for his plans? Give reasons for your answer.

   _____

   _____

2. In another story, Coyote steals fire to give to the people on Earth. In what ways would the two stories be alike?

   _____

   _____

43

Vocabulary Development

Using Categorizing

Categorizing is a way to help you figure out the meaning of words you do not know. Here is how categorizing works. Read the following sentence:

The Indians stored beans, squash, and <u>maize</u> for the winter.

Suppose the underlined word is a word you cannot read. This is what to do. Look at the other words that are listed along with the unknown word. Let's list them along with the unknown word. They are:

beans
squash
<u>maize</u>

Look at the list. You can read the first two words. Try to figure out what they have in common. How are these two words alike?

Beans and squash are both _____.

So, <u>maize</u> is probably a _____, too.

Read the sentences below. Write a definition for each underlined word.

1. Indians painted their drums with yellow, green, and russet designs.

   Think: Yellow and green are _____.

   So, <u>russet</u> is probably a _____, too.

2. The head of a drum is usually made of the skin of a goat, cow, or antelope.

   Think: Goats and cows are both _____.

   So, an <u>antelope</u> is probably an _____, too.

3. Some flutes, <u>xylophones</u>, and drums are made of wood.

   Think: Flutes and drums are _____.

   So, a <u>xylophone</u> is probably an _____, too.

Test Taking

Read the following passage. Then complete the items below by filling in the correct choices in the answer grid.

Some Indians made water drums. These drums were carved from logs and covered with deerskin. A hole and a plug were put on the side and water was poured into the drum. The amount of water changed the sound that the drum made.

1. This passage is mainly about
   a. where drums were made.
   b. why Indians made drums.
   c. how water drums were made.

2. All water drums had
   a. five sides.
   b. a high sound.
   c. a place to hold water.

3. You can tell that water drums
   a. were all alike.
   b. made different sounds.
   c. were played only by men.

	a	b	c		a	b	c		a	b	c
1.	△	△	△	2.	△	△	△	3.	△	△	△

Applying Your Skills

Some Indians painted their drums. Sometimes the pictures on the drum had to do with things in nature. Sometimes the picture told something about the drummer.

Design a drum you would like to have. Name its parts. Decorate your drum.

45

YOUR WONDERFUL HANDS

You use your hands for almost everything you do. Can you think of three things you do during the day that don't involve the use of your hands?
- Look at your hands. Can you touch each finger with your thumb?
- Why are your thumbs so important to your hands?

Turn off the alarm! Throw off the covers! It's time to get up! Now brush your teeth, get dressed, eat your breakfast. You do these things every day. There's nothing to it, right?

But wait a minute. Think about it. Think of all the different ways you use your hands to do these everyday things. Look at the shape of your hands. You couldn't do even the easiest things if they were a different shape. Imagine making a phone call if you had paws, or playing a musical instrument if you had flippers!

But you don't have paws or flippers. What you do have are two very complicated tools, one at the end of each of your arms. These tools are your hands. Each hand has twenty-six small bones that make it very flexible. Each hand has five digits; four of the digits are fingers, the other digit is what is called an opposable thumb.

The opposable thumb is used like another hand to grasp things. Try to pick up an object with the finger of one hand without using your thumb. Chances are that you will need to use your other hand to hold the object firmly. Watch the way a squirrel uses its paws to hold a nut. It often has to use both paws because the paws don't have opposable thumbs.

Because of the way you can move your thumbs, you are able to hold an object with one hand while you do something else, like fix the object, with the other. This is only one of the many things you can do because your hands have opposable thumbs.

flippers (FLIP urz)   the broad, flat limbs on some animals, such as seals and penguins.
complicated (KOM pluh kayt id)   not simple; intricate
flexible (FLEK suh bul)   able to bend easily
digits (DIJ its)   the main parts of hands and feet; fingers, thumbs, and toes
opposable (uh POH zuh bul)   able to be placed opposite to and to touch the fingers of the hand of which it is a part

Direct Recall

Circle the letter of the choice that best completes each sentence.

1. You use your hands
   a. for almost everything you do.   b. to do everything.   c. to do a few things.

2. In your hand there are
   a. twenty-six bones.   b. five bones.   c. fifteen bones.

3. Another word for fingers is
   a. tools   b. hooves.   c. digits.

4. Each of your hands has
   a. two digits.   b. four fingers and an opposable thumb.   c. a small brain.

5. To hold a nut, squirrels often use
   a. their thumbs.   b. both paws.   c. two digits.

Inferential Thinking

Circle the letter of the choice that best completes each item below.

1. One reason a squirrel could not use a knife and fork is because it
   a. has no opposable thumb.
   b. is too small.
   c. has too many digits.

2. Your hand is like a
   a. brain.
   b. digit.
   c. tool.

3. If your hands were less flexible, you couldn't
   a. point at things.
   b. play a guitar.
   c. clap them together.

4. Another good title for this selection is
   a. "How to Play a Guitar."
   b. "How Squirrels Eat."
   c. "The Opposable Thumb."

Critical Thinking

1. If a dog had an opposable thumb, how might it eat its food?

   _____

   _____

2. Think of a game you like to play. Could you play it if you didn't have an opposable thumb? Give reasons for your answer.

   _____

   _____

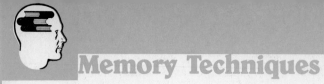

Memory Techniques

Taking Notes

Read the story below. Use the lines to take notes. Remember, you don't have to copy every word. Just write the important words. What are the main ideas in this story? What are the supporting ideas?

The human hand helps people talk. The American Indians used hand signals to talk to each other. Deaf people and their friends use their hands and fingers to form words and letters.

Hands tell feelings and ideas without words. Everyone knows the hand signals for "Stop" and "Be Quiet!" However, not all signals are given on purpose. You may clench your fists when you are angry or move your hands in special ways when you are upset.

Notes

Paragraph 1   Main Idea: _____

        Supporting Ideas: _____

_____

Paragraph 2   Main Idea: _____

        Supporting Ideas: _____

_____

_____

Test Taking

Read the following passage. Then complete the items below by filling in the correct choices in the answer grid.

Years ago, left-handed children were forced to use their right hand. Sometimes they were even punished for writing with their left hand. Today, children are not prevented from using their left hand if it is more comfortable for them. In fact, some tools, such as scissors, are made especially for left-handed people. Do you know that fifteen percent of all people are left-handed?

Some people can use one hand as well as the other. Researchers still don't know why this is so.

1. Left-handed children are
   a. punished.
   b. unusual.
   c. mostly girls.

2. A good title for this selection is
   a. "Left-handed Scissors."
   b. "Left Can Be Right."
   c. "Why Some People Are Left-Handed."

3. A fact that proves that being left-handed is perfectly acceptable today is that
   a. everyone is forced to use their left hands.
   b. most people are left-handed.
   c. some tools are made especially for left-handed people.

	a	b	c		a	b	c		a	b	c
1.	△	△	△	2.	△	△	△	3.	△	△	△

Applying Your Skills

Did you realize that the word *hand* is part of many words and phrases? Some examples are: *hand*•some, second•*hand*, lend a helping *hand*. List as many examples of *hand* words and phrases as you can.

_____

_____

_____

_____

_____

FAST FOODS

America's eating habits are changing. Fast-food and take-out restaurants are opening by the thousands all across the United States.
- What did you eat for dinner last night?
- Where did you eat it? Who cooked it?

Not long ago, most people would answer these questions by saying: "We had several courses for dinner last night. The whole family sat down together at the dinner table at around six o'clock. Cooking, eating, and cleaning up afterward took several hours.

Today, things have changed. Family members may have to eat at different times. They may even have to eat at different places. So, fast-food and take-out restaurants have sprung up all across the country.

Why have things changed? There are many reasons. For example, more women go to work today than in the past. Working full-time outside the home doesn't leave much time or energy for preparing meals.

Another reason that fast-food and take-out places are so popular is that there are more single-parent families today. The head of a single-parent family may find it impossible to work all day and then provide meals for his or her family.

People live longer today, and there are many elderly people who live alone. There are also young, single people who live alone. Many of these people don't like to bother cooking meals just for themselves. So they eat out in fast-food restaurants or buy take-out food.

Teenagers are big fast-food fans, too. Maybe because so many of their parents work, teenagers can eat what they want, when they want, and where they want. They like to spend time with their friends, and they often do this at fast-food places.

Many things have changed in the world since your parents were young. Eating habits are just one of those things.

fast-food (FAST FOOD)   specializing in food that is prepared and served quickly
take-out (TAYK out)   specializing in food that is to be taken out and eaten somewhere else
courses (KAWR sez)   different parts of a meal
energy (EN ur jee)   power to do work

Direct Recall

Circle the letter of the choice that best completes each sentence.

1. Just a few years ago, most families
   a. ate out every night.   b. ate at different times.   c. sat down together for a large dinner.

2. Cooking, eating, and cleaning up after dinner took
   a. one hour.   b. several minutes.   c. several hours.

3. Working full-time outside the home leaves little time and energy for
   a. preparing meals.   b. eating out.   c. buying fast food.

4. Today there are more
   a. elderly and single people who live alone.   b. children.   c. people who work at home.

5. Many teenagers today can
   a. choose what to eat.   b. go to fancy restaurants.   c. cook.

Inferential Thinking

Circle the letter of the choice that best completes each item below.

1. Many people prefer take-out food because it is
   a. less trouble.
   b. cheap.
   c. healthier.

2. You can conclude that the number of fast-food places
   a. will increase.
   b. will stay the same.
   c. will decrease.

3. Parents who buy fast foods may be
   a. too busy to cook.
   b. very rich.
   c. not very good cooks.

4. Another title for this selection might be
   a. "Hamburgers."
   b. "Why People Eat."
   c. "New Eating Habits."

Critical Thinking

1. Do you think that television helped fast-food and take-out places grow? Give reasons for your answer.

   _____

2. What changes would make your neighborhood fast-food restaurant better? What improvements would you like to see?

   _____

Vocabulary Development

Understanding Idioms

Idioms are ways to describe things. You use many idioms in your daily speech. They have become a part of the English language. Some of the idioms seem to refer to food, but they are really about feelings and ideas. Read the idioms below. Tell what each idiom really means on the line below.

1. I think she bit off more than she can chew.

_____

2. He's nutty as a fruitcake.

_____

3. I have a bone to pick with you.

_____

4. Don't cry over spilled milk.

_____

5. They sat around chewing the fat.

_____

Test Taking

Read the following paragraph. Then complete the items below. Fill in the answers in the answer grid.

You probably think that the way you eat is normal. You may think that the eating habits of people in other countries are odd. Asian people eat a lot of rice. In France, snails are a popular dish. Some people in India think it is terrible to eat beef. There are certain foods that people will not eat, no matter how hungry they are. The foods that people will or will not eat, however, are different in each country.

1. Asians eat a great deal of
   a. potatoes.   **b.** noodles.   **c.** rice.

2. If people are hungry enough, they will
   a. eat any kind of food.   **b.** still not eat certain foods.   **c.** eat normally.

3. It is important to remember that
   a. tastes are different.   **b.** all people are alike.   **c.** you should eat food you don't like.

	a	b	c		a	b	c		a	b	c
1.	△	△	△	**2.**	△	△	△	**3.**	△	△	△

Applying Your Skills

Design a menu for the meal you would most like to have. Check the courses you want. Tell how you want your food prepared.

A Menu for _____

☐ **First course** _____

☐ **Main dish** _____

☐ **Vegetable** _____

☐ **Salad** _____

☐ **Potatoes** _____

☐ **Drink** _____

☐ **Dessert** _____

WEST WITH THE WOMEN

What is the farthest you ever walked? One mile? Five miles? Ten miles? Try to imagine what it would be like to walk across the entire country.

- Do you think men were the only pioneers?
- How did the pioneer women live?

In the early days of our country, people heard how rich and beautiful the land was out west. Very few people went because the trip was long, hard, and dangerous.

Then, suddenly everything changed. In 1848, gold was discovered in California. Thousands of people headed west. Although some had caught "gold fever," others went for different reasons. The West was being opened up, and people had a chance to start a new life.

Many single women and widows got together and bought wagons and equipment. They joined wagon trains headed for the new land. They did everything the men did. When the wagon trains were in camp, they took care of their wagons and guarded the camp at night. When the wagon trains were crossing mountains or rivers, the women often couldn't ride. At those times, they walked alongside the wagons. They pushed their wagons through mud and pulled them across icy rivers. The trip was difficult and took many months. People died on the way.

When the trip was over, the pioneers had to work even harder. They built their houses out of whatever was on the land. They had to make everything they needed. There were no stores where they could buy things.

It was a hard life. Work began at dawn and didn't end until night. Everybody—men, women, and children—had to help clear the land and take care of the crops. In addition to doing these jobs, the women cooked, cleaned, made clothing, and raised the children. When it was necessary, they used rifles to protect their homes against unfriendly Indians and wild animals.

In order to survive when things were hardest, the pioneers needed courage and strength. The pioneer women had plenty of both.

dangerous (DAYN jer us) full of danger; risky
equipment (i KWIP munt) things that are needed when making a long trip
survive (sur VYV) to last through a dangerous time
courage (KUR ij) bravery

Direct Recall

Circle the letter of the choice that best completes each sentence.

1. Single women and widows
   a. had special jobs.   **b.** stayed in the East.   **c.** joined wagon trains.

2. The trip west took many
   a. days.   **b.** weeks.   **c.** months.

3. The pioneers built their houses out of
   a. wood.   **b.** whatever was on the land.   **c.** brick.

4. Before gold was found in California
   a. few people traveled west.   **b.** women bought wagons and equipment.
   c. many pioneers started farms.

5. Pioneer women
   a. had easy lives.   **b.** shared all the work with the men.   **c.** were never sick.

Inferential Thinking

1. What words do not describe pioneer women?
   a. Strong and independent
   b. Hard working
   c. Lazy and selfish

2. How do you think most women felt about their lives?
   a. They loved all the work.
   b. They wished life were easier.
   c. They wanted to return east.

3. People died on their way west because
   a. they were old.
   b. they were sickly.
   c. they were overcome by the hardships of the trip.

4. You can conclude that the pioneers
   a. went west to sightsee.
   b. went west in search of better lives.
   c. liked to live in cities.

Critical Thinking

1. What were some important qualities pioneers had to have? Give reasons for your answer.

2. People who traveled on the wagon trains are not alive today. How do you think so much is known about pioneer life?

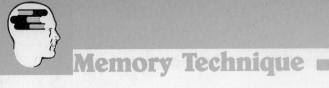

Using Questions to Recall Important Details

A good way to remember what you read is:

First, write the main idea of the story or article you
read. *What* is it about?
Then, list important details that support the main idea.

It may help to ask yourself questions such as: *who, what, when, why,* and *how.*

Read "West With the Woman" again. Fill in the chart below. The main idea is done for you.

Main Idea

Who or *What* is the story about? _____ Pioneer women _____

Important Details

When did they go? _____

Why did they go? _____

How did they go? _____

What happened when they got to the new land? _____

How did they live? _____

Test Taking

Read the following passage. Then complete the items below by filling in the correct choices in the answer grid.

There were few trees on the Great Plains, so the pioneers built what were called sod houses. Sod is another word for soil. They dug up earth and packed it into blocks. Then they piled the blocks one on top of another to make walls. They made the roofs out of straw. There were many problems. Dirt fell into their food and beds. Animals made tunnels through the walls and mice lived in the roof. Sod houses were not pleasant places in which to live.

1. To make sod houses, pioneers first had to
   a. pile up blocks of earth.
   b. dig up earth.
   c. make a straw roof.

2. Sod houses were not
   a. warm in winter.
   b. cool in summer.
   c. clean.

3. A good title for this article would be
   a. "Sod Houses of the Plains."
   b. "Blocks of Earth."
   c. "Why Sod Houses Were Built."

	a	b	c		a	b	c		a	b	c
1.	△	△	△	2.	△	△	△	3.	△	△	△

Applying Your Skill

Pretend you are a pioneer. You want your best friend from back east to come out west and stay with you. Write a letter to your friend telling all the good things about where you are and how you live. Try to talk your friend into moving west.

_____

_____

_____

_____

_____

_____

_____

_____

_____

_____

SOMEBODY

Althea Gibson always wanted to be somebody—even when, as a teenager she was fighting in the streets and cutting school. Even when her temper kept getting her into trouble, Althea Gibson wanted to be somebody.

- Have you ever heard of Althea Gibson?
- Why was her beautiful speech so important?

When Althea Gibson was young and living in Harlem, she was very poor. Luckily, sports activities were free. Althea liked sports and was very good at them. It didn't take long for people to notice how good she really was. Those people wanted to help Althea, so they gave her tennis lessons. Although Althea soon became a fine player, she was a bad sport and very rude. Even though she was learning a lot about tennis, she still had a lot to learn about herself.

In spite of her faults, people admired Althea's talent and continued to help her. They wanted her to be the best tennis player she could possibly be. They also wanted her to be the best person she could be. So, with their help, Althea studied and practiced.

By 1948, Althea Gibson was one of the best women tennis players in the United States. Then, in 1951, she became the first black athlete to play at Wimbledon. Wimbledon is a suburb of London, England, where international tennis matches are played. Althea was very nervous and didn't play well. When she lost the match, some people thought that Althea's career was finished. But she didn't quit. She fought her way back to the top rank of tennis players.

Finally in 1957, again at Wimbledon, Althea Gibson was crowned the best woman tennis player in the world! The queen of England congratulated her.

After winning, Althea spoke these words: "God grant that I may wear this crown with dignity, defend it with honor, and when my day is done, give it up graciously." Althea Gibson had indeed become somebody.

---

tennis (TEN is)   a game played by hitting a ball over a net to an opponent
congratulate (kun GRAT yoo layt)   to tell a person you are pleased with what he or she has done
dignity (DIG nih tee)   a noble, stately, honorable manner
honor (AHN ur)   great respect
graciously (GRAY shus lee)   with courtesy and kindness

Direct Recall

Circle the letter of the choice that best completes each sentence.

1. When she was young, Althea Gibson was
   a. a bad sport and very rude.   b. very shy and polite.   c. unhappy and very frightened.

2. By 1948, Althea Gibson was one of the best tennis players in
   a. the world.   b. England.   c. the United States.

3. Wimbledon is in
   a. Harlem.   b. England.   c. America.

4. The queen of England
   a. congratulated Althea.   b. played tennis with Althea.   c. was a good sport.

5. Althea wanted to wear the crown with
   a. honor.   b. dignity.   c. somebody.

Inferential Thinking

Circle the letter of the choice that best completes each item below.

1. Which statement below is a fact?
   a. Althea Gibson was the best tennis player that ever lived.
   b. She was crowned the best woman tennis player in the world at Wimbledon in 1957.
   c. Finally, everybody liked Althea Gibson.

2. You can conclude that she worked hard to
   a. improve herself as well as her tennis game.
   b. show the queen how well she could play tennis.
   c. be the most polite tennis player in the world.

3. Being the first black person to play at Wimbledon probably made
   a. no difference to Althea.
   b. Althea want to meet the queen.
   c. Althea nervous.

4. At the ball in her honor, Althea acted
   a. with pride and dignity.
   b. with tears and laughter.
   c. like a bad sport.

Critical Thinking

1. What did Althea mean when she said she "wanted to be somebody"?

   _____

2. What did Althea Gibson have to learn between 1951 and 1957?

   _____

Vocabulary Development

Understanding Prefixes

Prefixes are one or more letters put before the beginning of a word to change its meaning. The prefixes *un-* and *in-* mean "not."

Read the following sentence:

Althea Gibson was rude and unsporting.

"Sporting" means "like a good sport," so "*un*sporting" means "*not* like a good sport."

In the same way, "complete" means "finished," so "*in*complete" means "not finished."

Add the following prefixes to the words below. Then write sentences that show you understand what the new word means.

un-	in-
clear	active
even	sane
fair	dependent

	New Word	Sentence
1.	_____	_____
2.	_____	_____
3.	_____	_____
4.	_____	_____
5.	_____	_____
6.	_____	_____

Test Taking

Read the following passage. Then complete the items below by filling in the correct choices in the answer grid.

> The people who helped Althea knew that to become a great tennis player, she had to learn more than tennis. She had to learn how to control herself and her temper. She had to learn how to handle defeat. She had to learn how to stay cool when things were going badly. Only then could she become a great tennis player.

1. The author thinks that it takes more than playing well to be a
   a. great tennis player.
   b. black athlete.
   c. good sport.

2. A good title for this would be
   a. "Learning to be the Best."
   b. "How to Play Tennis."
   c. "People Who Helped Althea."

3. You can conclude that it was hard for Althea to
   a. control her temper.
   b. play tennis.
   c. get angry.

	a	b	c		a	b	c		a	b	c
1.	△	△	△	2.	△	△	△	3.	△	△	△

Applying Your Skills

In playing tennis, the idea is not only to hit the ball over the net. It is also to put the ball exactly where you want it to go. Draw a line from the sentence on the left side of the net to the correct ball on the right. The first one is done for you.

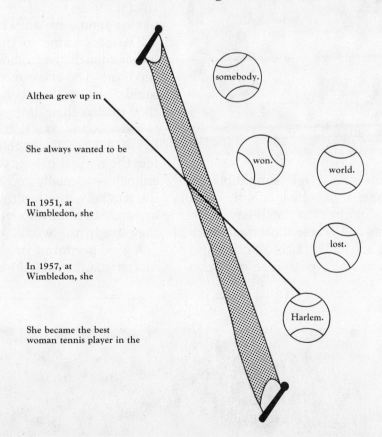

Althea grew up in

She always wanted to be

In 1951, at Wimbledon, she

In 1957, at Wimbledon, she

She became the best woman tennis player in the

somebody.

won.

world.

lost.

Harlem.

ZOOS TO THE RESCUE

Years ago, rich people collected strange animals and kept them in private parks. These were the first zoos. Later, public zoos were built for all people to enjoy.

- Do you care about animals?
- How have zoos changed in how they care for animals?

The first public zoos were simple places. The animals were kept behind bars in small cages. They had nothing to do all day. They looked at people and people looked at them. That was all. They had no trees to climb, no water to swim in, no caves to hide in. A zoo was just a place for people to stare at animals.

Then, things changed. Many kinds of wild animals started to die out. There were a number of reasons for this. People began to take over lands where animals lived. The animals were crowded together in smaller places and did not have enough food to survive. People shot animals for food and for their beautiful skins. They killed animals for sport. Also, people polluted the land and the water that wild animals depended on.

People began to worry: Would endangered animals, like pandas, elephants, and tigers, become extinct? When an animal becomes extinct it means that there are no more animals of that kind alive anywhere on earth.

The zoos came to the rescue. It was no longer enough just to show animals sitting behind bars. The endangered animals had to be saved. So many zoos changed the way in which they treated their animals.

Today, many zoos don't keep their animals in small cages. Good zoos are designed to be like the natural habitats of the animals. The animals—especially endangered animals—can live naturally, have healthy babies, and increase in number. At the same time, you can see how they live in the wild.

A good beginning has been made, but a lot more remains to be done.

private (PRY vit)   just for oneself
polluted (poh LOO ted)   not healthy; poisoned
endangered (en DAYN jerd)   unprotected; to be in peril
extinct (eks TINGT)   die out; no longer exist
habitat (HAB i tat)   the place where an animal lives or grows
naturally (NAT choo ral ee)   in a natural manner; by nature

Direct Recall

Circle the letter of the choice that best completes each sentence.

1. Extinction lasts
   a. for a very long time.   b. forever.   c. until new babies are born.

2. Natural habitats are
   a. foods.   b. habits.   c. places to live.

3. Good zoos try to save
   a. wildlife.   b. money.   c. time.

4. To save endangered species, many zoos have
   a. put animals in cages.   b. let animals go.   c. built natural habitats.

5. Pandas, elephants, and tigers
   a. are endangered animals.   b. live in zoos.   c. make good pets.

Inferential Thinking

Circle the letter of the choice that best completes each item below.

1. You can conclude that the worst enemy of all animals is
   a. other animals.
   b. big game hunters.
   c. people.

2. When an animal becomes extinct, it
   a. has only a few babies.
   b. doesn't exist anymore.
   c. changes into something else.

3. If many people wore coats of tiger fur, tigers might
   a. be kept alive.
   b. become extinct.
   c. need special foods.

4. This article is mainly about
   a. saving wildlife.
   b. how pollution kills animals.
   c. how zoos began.

Critical Thinking

1. Do you think there should be a law against killing animals for food? Explain your answer.

_____

2. Do you think there should be a law against killing animals for their skin? Explain your answer.

_____

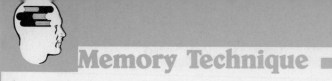

Memory Technique

Using Questions to Recall Important Details

A good way to remember what you read is:

> First, write the main idea of your story or article. What is it about?
> Then list important details that support the main idea.

It will help to ask yourself questions such as: *who, what, why, when,* and *how.*

Read "Zoos to the Rescue" again. Fill in the chart below.

Main Idea:

Who or *What* is this article about? _____

_____

Important Details:

What were the first zoos like? _____

_____

Why did animals become endangered? _____

_____

What does *extinct* mean? _____

_____

How have zoos changed? _____

_____

Test Taking

Read the following passage. Then complete the items below by filling in the correct choices in the answer grid.

When the Indians hunted buffalo with bow and arrow, the size of the herds stayed about the same. When the white men began hunting, they used guns and rifles. They killed so many buffaloes that the animal almost became extinct. The Bronx Zoo decided to save them. It took years of careful work, but the zoo succeeded. Today, there are many healthy herds of buffalo in the United States and Canada.

1. When only Indians hunted buffalo, the herd size
   a. got larger.   **b.** got smaller.   **c.** stayed about the same.

2. Buffaloes became endangered after hunters began using
   a. bows and arrows.   **b.** guns and rifles.   **c.** spears.

3. A good title for this selection is
   a. "Saving the Buffalo."   **b.** "Buffalo Bill."   **c.** "An Extinct Animal."

	a	b	c		a	b	c		a	b	c
1.	△	△	△	**2.**	△	△	△	**3.**	△	△	△

Applying Your Skills

There are many animals that we know of that do not exist. Some of these animals, like dragons, probably never did exist. Other animals, like dinosaurs, became extinct through natural causes. Some animals, like the dodo, are extinct because of people. Draw as many animals as you can that do not exist. Include both animals that never did exist and animals that have become extinct.

THE BAKER'S DAUGHTER

Folk stories and tales of magic have been told for many years. Often in these stories, people are punished by being turned into animals or birds.

- How is good rewarded in this story?
- What happened to the greedy daughter?

In a certain town long ago, there lived a baker who had two daughters. One was generous and kind. The other was greedy and mean.

One cold winter night, the good daughter was alone in the bakery when an old ragged woman came in. She said she was hungry and asked for some bread. "Of course," said the girl and put some dough in the oven to bake.

The old woman sat down nearby and seemed to sleep. "She must be very tired," thought the girl, and gently put a pillow behind the old woman's head. When the girl took the bread out of the oven, she cried out in surprize. The bread was twice as big as usual.

The old woman changed into a beautiful fairy and said, "Because you have a good heart, your bread will always double in size."

Many nights later, the old woman came in to the shop again. This time the greedy daughter was there. When the old woman asked for a piece of bread, the girl reluctantly broke off a tiny bit of dough and put it in the oven. Again, the old woman seemed to doze off. When the girl took the bread out of the oven, she also was surprized. The bread was so big and shiny and beautiful! She grabbed the loaf and hid it away for herself.

"Is the bread ready yet?" asked the old woman. She pretended to be waking up.

"Oh, I'm so sorry. It burned before I could take it out of the oven," said the greedy girl. "Hoo, hoo," she laughed. "I guess you will have to go without bread."

"Hoo, hoo, indeed," said the old woman as she turned again into a beautiful fairy. "Because you were greedy and lied to me, from now on you will always say "Whoo, whoo." And with that she changed the greedy girl into an owl.

And so the baker's greedy daughter remained an owl forever, always crying, "Whoo, whoo."

generous (JEN ur us)   willing to give or share
greedy (GREE dee)   selfish
dough (DOH)   flour, water, and yeast for making bread
double (DUB l)   become twice as big as usual
reluctantly (ree LUK tant lee)   not wanting to

Direct Recall

Circle the letter of the choice that best completes each sentence.

1. The baker's daughters were very
   a. different. **b.** poor. **c.** pretty.

2. The old woman asked for
   a. a place to sleep. **b.** money. **c.** bread.

3. The old woman was really
   a. an evil witch. **b.** a beautiful fairy. **c.** a poor beggar.

4. The greedy daughter wanted the bread
   a. for herself. **b.** for her sister. **c.** for the old woman.

5. The greedy daughter said that the loaf was
   a. too big. **b.** burned. **c.** not ready.

Inferential Thinking

Circle the letter of the choice that best completes each item below.

1. The old woman acted as if she were asleep so that
   a. she could watch the girls.
   b. no one would bother her.
   c. the bread would be finished.

2. The old woman pretended to be poor because
   a. it was an easy way to travel.
   b. she wanted to see how the girls would treat her.
   c. she was really hungry.

3. The good daughter was rewarded for being
   a. careful and tidy.
   b. generous and kind.
   c. making a fine loaf of bread.

4. The breads were so large and delicious because the
   a. dough was well mixed.
   b. fairy did it by magic.
   c. daughters were good bakers.

Critical Thinking

1. This story teaches a familiar lesson. What lesson does it teach?

   _____

2. The old woman tricked the girls. She pretended to be asleep. Do you think that was fair? Give reasons for your answer.

   _____

Vocabulary Development

Understanding Antonymns

Antonyms are words that have opposite meanings. For example, the words *sleep* and *wake* are antonyms.

Read the sentences below. Circle the letter of the word that is opposite in meaning to the underlined word. Write the correct word in the blank in each sentence.

1. The two girls were not <u>similar</u>. They were _____.
   a. shy.   **b.** different.   **c.** proud.

2. One girl was <u>generous</u>, the other was _____.
   a. careful.   **b.** mean.   **c.** selfish.

3. One girl was <u>rude</u>, the other was _____.
   a. polite.   **b.** angry.   **c.** loud.

4. The <u>clever</u> fairy was not at all _____.
   a. sorry.   **b.** polite.   **c.** stupid.

5. The owl is a <u>wild</u> bird. It is never very _____.
   a. shy.   **b.** tame.   **c.** fierce.

6. This story is not <u>new</u>. It is very _____.
   a. old.   **b.** popular.   **c.** true.

Test Taking

Read the following passage. Then complete the sentences. Fill in the correct answers in the answer grid.

> The owl usually lives alone and hunts for food at night. Owls can fly fast. They are birds of prey who kill and eat other animals such as mice and rats. You can recognize an owl by the feathers it has around its eyes. The owl's eyes are very large. Owls look wiser than other birds. In fact, geese, crows, and ravens are all smarter than owls.

1. You can conclude that owls
  a. can see well at night.
  b. can see well during the day.
  c. sleep only at night.

2. An owl is
  a. smarter than a dog.
  b. not as smart as a crow.
  c. a very wise bird.

3. A bird of prey is a bird that
  a. eats plants.
  b. eats other animals.
  c. has feathers around its eyes.

	a	b	c		a	b	c		a	b	c
1.	△	△	△	**2.**	△	△	△	**3.**	△	△	△

Testing Your Skills

Read the sentence below. Write as many questions as you can. The word *owl* should be the correct answer to all your questions. One question is done for you.

The answer is *owl.*

1. What animal was the baker's daughter turned into?

2. _____

3. _____

4. _____

5. _____

6. _____

PICTURE THIS!

For years, people have argued about whether the Lake Champlain monster is real or not. Now, someone has taken a picture of it.
- What would you do if you saw a monster in a lake?
- What other monsters have you heard of?

There is a legend about a monster in Lake Champlain. People call the monster Champ.

Lake Champlain is a large lake between Vermont and New York. It is 125 miles long and about 14 miles wide. In some places, it is 400 feet deep.

The Lake is named after Samuel de Champlain, a French explorer who discovered it in 1609. When de Champlain explored the lake, he reported seeing a monster with a long neck and humps that stuck out of the water. It was then that the legend of Champ began.

Since that time, other people have claimed that they, too, have seen Champ. But for every person who believes in the monster, there is one or more who doubt its existence. The doubters say that the monster is really only a log or just a big fish.

It is hard, however, to say this to a woman named Sandra Mansi, because she has taken a picture of the monster!

One day Mrs. Mansi and her family were having a picnic on the shore of Lake Champlain. All of a sudden, Mrs. Mansi saw a large head and a long neck come up from the lake. She quickly picked up her camera and took a picture of the creature.

Many scientists have studied the picture Mrs. Mansi took. Some of them believe that Champ may be a prehistoric cousin of whales. They think that Champ and other animals like Champ swam up rivers from the sea thousands of years ago hunting for fish. These animals got trapped and could not return to the sea. Now, they live in large lakes like Lake Champlain.

Other scientists feel that Champ may be a kind of dinosaur. Still others are certain that the thing that Mrs. Mansi photographed was not a living creature at all.

There is only one thing that everybody can agree on. No one will know the truth about Champ—if there *is* a Champ—unless whatever it is can be caught and examined.

creature (KREE chur)   a living being
prehistoric (pree his TAWR ik)   of the time before people wrote history
dinosaur (DY nuh sawr)   a large animal that lived millions of years ago
examined (eg ZAM und)   looked at carefully

70

Direct Recall

Circle the letter of the choice that best completes each sentence.

1. Lake Champlain is
   a. in Vermont.   **b.** in New York.   **c.** between Vermont and New York.

2. Samuel de Champlain reported seeing a monster in
   a. 1609.   **b.** 1492.   **c.** 1906.

3. While some people say they have seen Champ, others say
   a. it is a dinosaur or a whale.   **b.** the photograph is too fuzzy.   **c.** it is a log or a big fish.

4. On the shore of Lake Champlain one day, Mrs. Mansi and her family were
   a. having a picnic.   **b.** talking about Champ.   **c.** taking pictures.

5. Some scientists think Champ may be a
   a. kind of eagle.   **b.** cousin of the whale.   **c.** submarine.

Inferential Thinking

Circle the letter of the choice that best completes each item below.

1. Some people probably don't think there is a monster because
   a. the water is too deep.
   b. there has never been any real proof.
   c. Mrs. Mansi is not a scientist.

2. When Mrs. Mansi thought she saw Champ, she first thought about
   a. recording his existence with a camera.
   b. becoming famous.
   c. helping scientists.

3. You can conclude that scientists
   a. don't care about Champ.
   b. agree about Champ.
   c. don't agree about Champ.

4. Another title for this article could be
   a. "Samuel de Champlain."
   b. "The Mystery of Champ."
   c. "Beautiful Lake Champlain."

Critical Thinking

1. If there *is* a monster in Lake Champlain, why do you think more people haven't seen it? Give reasons for your answer.

   _____

2. If there *isn't* a monster in Lake Champlain, why do people think they have seen it?

   _____

An Outline Is a List of Facts or Ideas

Read the two paragraphs below. Then, complete the outline by filling in your notes. First, write the main idea of each paragraph. Then, write the details that support the main idea. Some of the outline has been done for you.

Some people say there have been many Champs over the years. One reason they say this is because the monster cannot have lived for over 300 years. It would have gotten old and died, like other animals. This would mean that there are families of monsters with children.

Recently people have reported seeing more than one monster at a time. A man saw two swimming together. Maybe they were a male and female. A woman said she saw two swimming together near the shore. One was big and the other was very small. Perhaps she saw a mother and a baby Champ.

OUTLINE

Main Idea: _____

Details: _____

_____

Main Idea: _____

Details: _____

_____

Test Taking

Port Kent is a village on Lake Champlain. The people who live there call it "The Home of the Champ." There is a sign posted there with the names of people who have reported seeing Champ near there. The people of Port Kent sell T-shirts, bumper stickers, and buttons with drawings of Champ. Visitors from all over the world come to Port Kent hoping that they, too, will see the famous monster of Lake Champlain.

1. The Home of Champ is a
   a. city on Lake Champlain.
   b. country on Lake Champlain.
   c. village on Lake Champlain.

2. The people of Port Kent sell T-shirts, bumper stickers, and buttons with
   a. a picture of Lake Champlain.
   b. drawings of Champ.
   c. a picture of Mrs. Mansi.

3. People from all over the world think they will see Champ if they come to Port Kent because
   a. a lot of people have reported seeing Champ near there.
   b. Champ has a big, beautiful swimming pool there.
   c. Champ's picture is on bumper stickers and buttons.

	a	b	c		a	b	c		a	b	c
1.	△	△	△	2.	△	△	△	3.	△	△	△

Applying Your Skills

Pretend you own a hotel in Port Kent. Write an ad to get people to come and stay at your hotel.

_____

_____

_____

_____

_____

_____

_____

_____

_____

_____

_____

73

THE ONE-CHILD FAMILY IN CHINA

In 1979, the population of the People's Republic of China was reaching close to one billion. The Chinese government was afraid that there wouldn't be room for so many people and that there wouldn't be enough food to feed them.

- What did the Chinese government decide to do about this problem?
- What is the one-child policy?

The population of China was close to one billion. And it was growing fast. The Chinese leaders decided something had to be done. They started the one-child policy.

Young married people were told that they should have only one child. If they followed this policy, the population of China would not keep growing so fast. However, there is a long tradition among the Chinese people of having large families. Therefore, it was very hard for all of the Chinese people to accept the one-child policy.

However, many Chinese people have accepted it. There are 337 million children in China under the age of 14. Thirty million of these children have no brothers or sisters. The government rewards people who stick to the one-child policy. There are penalties for those who don't.

The one-child policy has helped to slow the population growth in China. However, a problem has come up that nobody had thought of. Some people in China feel that a lot of the children in one-child families are growing up spoiled and lazy. The Chinese people love children. They are used to having large families. In a one-child family, the child gets the attention not only of both parents but also of all the grandparents.

Some Chinese people think that so much attention may not be good for the children. The children sometimes behave badly. Sometimes, they throw tantrums. Something may have to be done about that.

---

population (pop yuh LAY shun)   number of people living in a place
policy (POL uh see)   a plan or course of action
reward (rih WARD)   something given for doing something or for completing a task or service
penalties (PEN uhl teez)   punishments

Direct Recall

Circle the letter of the choice that best completes each sentence.

1. In 1979, the population of China was close to
   a. one million.   **b.** one billion.   **c.** one trillion.

2. Young married people were told they should
   a. not have children.   **b.** have as many children as they wanted.   **c.** have only one child.

3. There are 337 million children in China
   a. with no brothers and sisters.   **b.** in one-child families.   **c.** under the age of 14.

4. The government gives rewards to people who
   a. have only one child.   **b.** have many children.   **c.** do not stick to the one-child policy.

5. Some people think the one-child policy
   a. has no problems.   **b.** has created spoiled children.   **c.** has created well-behaved children.

Inferential Thinking

Circle the letter of the choice that best completes each item below.

1. The Chinese leaders started the one-child policy because
   a. they did not like children.
   b. their population was growing too fast.
   c. their population was growing slowly.

2. You can conclude that in China there are
   a. not many one-child families.
   b. many one-child families.
   c. no one-child families.

3. The one-child policy was hard for the Chinese people to accept because they have a history
   a. of large families.
   b. of small families.
   c. of one-child families.

4. Spoiled children were an
   a. exciting result of the one-child family.
   b. expected result of the one-child family.
   c. unexpected result of the one-child family.

Critical Thinking

1. How would you describe a spoiled child?

   _____

2. Do you think that an only child is sometimes more spoiled than children with brothers and sisters? Give reasons for your answer.

   _____

Vocabulary Development

Understanding Antonyms

Antonyms are words that have opposite meanings. In the reading selection, you learn that the population of China was growing fast. The opposite of *fast* is *slowly*. The words *fast* and *slowly* are antonyms.

The words on the left were all taken from the story, "The One-Child Family in China." Find an antonym in the column on the right for each word. Draw a line from each word to its antonym.

1.	young	shrink
2.	close	followers
3.	large	somebody
4.	hard	solution
5.	grow	old
6.	leaders	penalties
7.	problem	far
8.	nobody	reject
9.	accept	easy
10.	rewards	small

Test Taking

Read the following passage. Then complete the items below by filling in the correct choices in the answer grid.

> The one-child family policy in China is having some success. But most of that success is taking place in the cities. Many people in the countryside find the one-child policy impossible. Farmers need children to help with work in the fields. First, the government tells the people to have only one child. Then, the government tells them to grow more food in the fields. The farmers say they can't do both. Therefore, many farmers are continuing to have large families.

1. Most of the one-child families are in
   a. the cities.
   b. the countryside.
   c. both the cities and the countryside.

2. Farmers
   a. need children to work in the fields.
   b. are in favor of one-child families.
   c. live in the cities.

3. Which statement is *not* true?
   a. Most large families are in the countryside.
   b. The government wants one-child families.
   c. The one-child family policy is having no success.

	a	b	c		a	b	c		a	b	c
1.	△	△	△	2.	△	△	△	3.	△	△	△

Applying Your Skills

Look at the cartoon below. What does it say about the one-child family in China?

THE SEDITION ACT OF 1798

Matthew Lyon was a member of congress from Vermont. He was arrested and jailed for criticizing the government.
- What was the Sedition Act of 1798?
- Are people in the United States allowed to criticize their government?

The Sedition Act of 1798 said that it was against the law for American citizens to say or write bad things about the government.

The party in charge of the government at that time was called the Federalist Party. The Republican Party, which was in opposition to the Federalists, was hoping to win the next election in 1800. The Republican candidate for president was Thomas Jefferson.

The Federalists used the Sedition Act to try to keep the Republicans from criticizing them. The law prohibited people from saying or writing anything bad about the government. Because of this, the Federalists thought that the Republicans would have a lot of trouble beating them in the next election.

Matthew Lyon, a Republican congressman who was running for reelection, was sent to jail because he criticized the government. Twenty-five other Republicans were arrested, ten were sentenced to prison.

The Federalists thought that their use of the Sedition Act would help them win the election. It turned out that they were wrong. The American people have always believed in freedom of speech. It's not surprising that many Americans were quite upset with what the Federalists were doing.

In the election of 1800, Matthew Lyon was reelected to congress while still in jail. Thomas Jefferson was elected the next president. He took up his duties in 1801, a year that marked the end of the Sedition Act.

---

sedition (sih DISH un)   speech or writing that makes people angry with their government
criticize (KRIT uh syz)   say bad things about; find fault with
election (ih LEK shun)   the process of choosing people by voting
reelected (ree ih LEKT id)   elected again
sentenced (SEN tunst)   to pronounce judgment or punishment upon

Direct Recall

Circle the letter of the choice that best completes each sentence.

1. The Sedition Act of 1798 said it was against the law to
   a. steal from the government.   b. write about the government.
   c. say or write bad things about the government.

2. The party in power in the government in 1798 was the
   a. Federalist Party.   b. Republican Party.   c. Democratic Party.

3. The Republicans wanted Thomas Jefferson for
   a. congress.   b. the Federalist Party.   c. president.

4. Matthew Lyon was sent to jail because he
   a. was a member of congress.   b. criticized the government.   c. came from Vermont.

5. The Federalists thought the Sedition Act would help them
   a. elect Thomas Jefferson.   b. win the election.   c. say bad things about the goverment.

Inferential Thinking

Circle the letter of the choice that best completes each item below.

1. You can conclude that Thomas Jefferson was
   a. a Federalist.
   b. a Republican.
   c. a Democrat.

2. Thomas Jefferson probably
   a. liked the Sedition Act of 1798.
   b. did not care about the Sedition Act.
   c. hated the Sedition Act of 1798.

3. You can conclude that the Federalists
   a. won the election of 1800.
   b. did not win the election of 1800.
   c. did not want to win the election of 1800.

4. Which statement is an opinion?
   a. The Sedition Act of 1798 was unfair.
   b. The Sedition Act was passed in 1798.
   c. Matthew Lyon went to jail.

Critical Thinking

1. Do you think people should go to jail for saying what they believe? Give reasons for your answer.

   _____

2. Do you think there is ever a time when people should be stopped from criticizing the government? Give reasons for your answer.

   _____

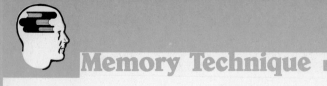

Memory Technique

Taking Notes

Taking notes is a helpful way to remember information. When you take notes on a reading selection, for example, write down only the important words. You don't need words like "a" and "the." You don't need to write in complete sentences when you take notes.

Read the following sentence:

Matthew Lyon was a member of congress from Vermont.

If you were taking notes, all you would need is:

Matthew Lyon—congress Vermont

Read the sentences below. They all come from the selection "The Sedition Act of 1798." Take notes on each sentence. Remember you are just writing down the key words.

1. He was arrested and sent to jail for criticizing his government.

_____

2. The party in charge of the government at that time was called the Federalist Party.

_____

3. The Federalists thought the Sedition Act would help them win the election.

_____

4. The American people have always believed in freedom of speech.

_____

5. It is not surprising that many Americans were quite upset.

_____

Test Taking

Read the following passage. Then complete the items below by filling in the correct choices in the answer grid.

> The United States government has *passed* sedition acts many times. There were acts *limiting* freedom of speech during the Civil War, World War I, and World War II. Governments often limit freedom of speech during wartime. Some people think it might be dangerous to allow people criticize the government during a war. The Sedition Act of 1798 was *unusual*. It was passed to help win an election, not to help win a war.

1. You can conclude that the word *passed* in this selection means
   a. thrown.
   b. moved ahead of.
   c. voted for.

2. You can conclude from the reading that the word *limiting* means
   a. making less.
   b. giving more.
   c. making better.

3. The word *unusual* means
   a. common.
   b. not common.
   c. not interesting.

	a	b	c		a	b	c		a	b	c
1.	△	△	△	2.	△	△	△	3.	△	△	△

Applying Your Skills

The words below are written in a secret code. Once a letter is written down, it is never written again. For example, the word *cobblestone* would be written *coblestn*.

Figure out what each word is. Then write it in the space below. All of the words were used in the reading selection. "The Sedition Act of 1798." The first one is done for you.

1. ARESTD _____arrested_____

2. GOVERNMT _____

3. CRITZE _____

4. SENTCD _____

5. BELIVD _____

6. RELCTD _____

81

ROMARE BEARDEN

You may think of collages as pictures made mostly by children in school. Romare Bearden, a famous black American artist, made collages that hang in museums around the country.
- What is a collage?
- What would you put in a collage?

Children in art class sometimes take things like pieces of colored paper and photographs from magazines and paste them onto a sheet of paper to make a picture. Romare Bearden was an artist who made serious works of art by doing something very similar. The works he made were collages.

Romare Bearden was a man with a lot of different interests. He wrote songs. Twenty of his songs were recorded. He played baseball.

He was a pitcher on his college varsity team. He also played in the summers for the Boston Tigers in an all-black baseball league.

Bearden went to college to become a doctor. While he was in college, however, he changed his mind. He started drawing cartoons for the *Afro-American*, a school newspaper. Bearden decided he liked making works of art better than writing songs, better than playing baseball, and better than becoming a doctor.

Romare Bearden started his art career as a painter. His work was soon admired by many people.

One day, Bearden went to a meeting with a group of other artists. He brought various materials such as pieces of colored paper and photographs with him. He had an idea that the whole group could work together to make a picture out of the different materials. It turned out that nobody was interested in the idea except Bearden himself. So he took the materials he had brought to the meeting back home and started to experiment. Soon his experimenting paid off. Romare Bearden had found the kind of art that he wanted to produce. He spent the rest of his life making collages.

collage (kuh LAHZH)   a work of art made by pasting materials on a surface
photographs (FOHT uh grafs)   pictures taken with a camera
varsity (VAHR suh tee)   the main team that plays for a school in a competition
league (LEEG)   a group of sports teams that play against one another
experiment (ik SPER uh munt)   to try something; to test out

Direct Recall

Circle the letter of the choice that best completes each sentence.

1. Romare Bearden had
   a. 20 songs recorded.   **b.** 30 songs recorded.   **c.** no songs recorded.

2. Romare Bearden played baseball as a
   a. first baseman.   **b.** pitcher.   **c.** catcher.

3. Bearden went to college to become
   a. an artist.   **b.** a lawyer.   **c.** a doctor.

4. He drew cartoons for *Afro-American*, a
   a. magazine.   **b.** school newspaper.   **c.** city newspaper.

5. When Bearden brought the various materials to the artists' meeting,
   a. everybody made a collage together.   **b.** the artists thought he had a great idea.
   c. he ended up bringing everything home and starting to experiment.

Inferential Thinking

Circle the letter of the choice that best completes each item below.

1. Which word best describes Romare Bearden?
   a. talented
   b. uninterested
   c. lazy

2. You can conclude that Romare Bearden's favorite form of art was probably
   a. the cartoon.
   b. the collage.
   c. painting.

3. Which statement is an opinion?
   a. Romare Bearden was a baseball player.
   b. Romare Bearden was an artist.
   c. Romare Bearden was a great artist.

4. Another good title for this selection is
   a. "The Boston Tigers."
   b. "Becoming a Painter."
   c. "Collage Artist."

Critical Thinking

1. If you could write songs, play baseball, become a doctor, or become an artist, which do you think you would choose? Give reasons for your answer.

2. Many of Romare Bearden's collages are hanging in museums. Why do you think people like to go to museums to see works of art?

Vocabulary Development

Forming Compound Words

In the reading selection, you read the word *baseball*. *Baseball* is a *compound word*. *Compound words* are formed by joining two words together to make a new word. The word *baseball* is made by joining the words *base* and *ball*.

Read the words in the two columns below. Draw a line between the words in the first and second columns that can be joined together to make compound words. The first one is done for you.

1. six   body
2. book   ache
3. lip   teen
4. class   coat
5. over   sauce
6. head   mat
7. some   case
8. door   writer
9. type   room
10. apple   stick

Test Taking

Read the following passage. Then complete the items below by filling in the correct choices in the answer grid.

A collage is a picture made up entirely or partly of pieces of paper, cloth or other material. The materials are pasted onto a surface. Artists use many different kinds of materials to make collages. Newspapers, photographs, bottle labels, and ticket stubs are just a few possibilities. Pablo Picasso and Georges Braque are two of the first world-famous artists who made collages.

1. The materials in a collage are
   a. pasted onto a surface.
   b. molded into a piece of clay.
   c. made with paints.

2. When making collages, artists
   a. always use photographs.
   b. must use cloth.
   c. use many different materials.

3. Pablo Picasso and Georges Braque
   a. are the only artists who made collages.
   b. are two of the first artists who made collages.
   c. did not make collages.

Applying Your Skills

Read the clues below, and fill in the correct words in the crossword puzzle. All of the answers are in the story "Romare Bearden."

Across
2. a work of art made by pasting materials onto a surface
5. try out; test
6. pictures taken with a camera

Down
1. the main team that plays for a school in a competition
3. the baseball position Romare Bearden played
4. group of sports teams that play against one another.

85

THE ERIE CANAL

In 1817, workers in New York State began digging a canal that would join Lake Erie and the Hudson River.
- What was the Erie Canal?
- Why was it so important?

In the early 1800s, most of the crops in the United States were grown in the West. Most of the cities were in the East. The Appalachian Mountains separated the two parts of the country. The people in the East needed food from the western farms. People in the West needed manufactured goods from eastern factories. Travel between East and West was very difficult.

For years, people dreamed of a waterway that would join the two parts of the country. But most people thought it would be an impossible task. How could they build a canal through the mountains? Then, in 1817, a man named DeWitt Clinton became the governor of New York. Governor Clinton had no idea how to build a canal. All he knew was that New York State needed one. He set aside money to build a canal and hired engineers to start working on a plan to build it. Many people laughed at Clinton. They didn't think it was possible to build a 350-mile canal. They called the canal "Clinton's Ditch."

But DeWitt Clinton was a man filled with optimism. He believed that people could do anything if they really wanted to. A group of engineers who had never built a canal planned a wonderful waterway. They invented machines for pulling out trees and cutting through the earth. Workers spent 14 hours a day at their labor. Together, the engineers and workers finished the impossible task.

In 1825, the Erie Canal was completed. It joined the farms of the West to the cities of the East. From that time on, nobody ever called the canal "Clinton's Ditch."

waterway (WAW tur way)   a water route that ships and boats can travel through
manufactured (man yuh FAK churd)   made, especially by machines
optimism (OP tuh miz um)   the belief that everything will be fine
invented (in VEN tid)   made for the first time
labor (LAY bur)   work

Direct Recall

Circle the letter of the choice that best completes each sentence.

1. In 1817, most of the cities in the United States were in
   a. the East. **b.** the West. **c.** the South.

2. The western farmers needed
   a. crops. **b.** manufactured goods. **c.** food.

3. DeWitt Clinton was
   a. president of the United States. **b.** mayor of New York. **c.** governor of New York.

4. Clinton believed that people
   a. could not build a 350-mile canal. **b.** were not very smart. **c.** could do anything.

5. The engineeers who planned the Erie Canal
   a. had built many canals before. **b.** had not built a canal before. **c.** could not build canals.

Inferential Thinking

Circle the letter of the choice that best completes each item below.

1. You can conclude that, in 1817, crossing the Appalachian Mountains was
   a. easy
   b. difficult.
   c. common.

2. You can conclude that the word *task* means
   a. job.
   b. canal.
   c. ditch.

3. Which words best describe the people who built the Erie Canal?
   a. smart and hard working
   b. stupid and hard working
   c. smart and lazy

4. The Erie Canal was completed in
   a. 1817.
   b. 1820.
   c. 1825.

Critical Thinking

1. In the reading selection, DeWitt Clinton is described as "a man filled with optimism." Explain what this means.

_____

2. Do you think you are a person with optimism? Give reasons for your answer.

_____

Memory Technique

Listing Events in Chronological Order

Chronological order is the order in which things happened. It is sometimes easier to remember information if you list events in chronological order.

Read the sentences below. Reread "The Erie Canal." Then rewrite the sentences in chronological order.

The engineers and workers spent eight years building the Erie Canal.

DeWitt Clinton became governor of New York State.

The farms of the West and the cities of the East were finally joined.

For years, people dreamed of a waterway that would join the East and the West.

Clinton set aside money and hired engineers to build a canal.

1. _____

2. _____

3. _____

4. _____

5. _____

Test Taking

Read the following passage. Then complete the items below by filling in the correct choices in the answer grid.

The United States has continued to be a country with a spirit of optimism. Almost 150 years after DeWitt Clinton set out to build a canal that couldn't be built, President John F. Kennedy promised to put a man on the moon. Nobody knew how to put a man on the moon, but that didn't stop Kennedy. Like Clinton before him, Kennedy put aside money and hired scientists to start working. In 1969, the first Americans landed on the moon.

1. President John F. Kennedy promised
   a. to build a great canal.
   b. to put a man on the moon.
   c. to build the first satellite.

2. The first Americans landed on the moon
   a. 150 years ago.
   b. in 1960.
   c. in 1969.

3. A good title for this selection would be
   a. "American Optimism."
   b. "John F. Kennedy."
   c. "The Moon."

	a	b	c		a	b	c		a	b	c
1.	△	△	△	2.	△	△	△	3.	△	△	△

Applying Your Skills

Look at the words *Erie Canal.* Use the space below to write as many words as you can think of using the letters in *Erie Canal.*

ERIE CANAL

_____

_____

_____

_____

_____

_____

GETTING COMMON SENSE

There are stories about getting knowledge in the folk tales of people all around the world. This Jamaican tale tells the story of Anansi, a young man who tried to gather together all the common sense there is.

- What is common sense?
- What does Anansi want to do with the common sense?

One day, Anansi had an idea. He decided that he would gather together all the common sense in the world. Then, people would need to come to him for help whenever they had problems. Anansi would charge lots of money for his advice. Soon, he would become very rich.

Anansi went around the world looking for common sense. He put every bit he could find into a large bag. When he finally could not find any more common sense to put into the bag, Anansi took the bag and went home. He decided to hide the bag at the very top of a tall tree.

Anansi tied the bag with a rope. He put the rope around his neck. The bag hung down in front of his body. Then, Anansi started to climb the tree. He had a terrible time climbing. The bag kept getting in his way.

Suddenly, Anansi heard a small boy's voice at the bottom of the tree. "Don't you think it would be easier if you put the bag on your back?" asked the boy.

Anansi couldn't believe his ears. Of course, the boy was right. Common sense tells you that it's easier to climb a tree with a bag on your back instead of on your front. Anansi got very angry. How could that small boy have so much common sense? Hadn't Anansi just gone around the world and gathered up all of the common sense there was?

Anansi took the bag, ripped it up, and threw its contents into the wind. The common sense scattered all over the world. Everybody got some of it, but nobody got all of it.

knowledge (NOL ij) information that is known
tale (TAYL) a story
gather (GATH ur) get and bring together
advice (ad VYS) an opinion about what someone should do
scattered (SKAT urd) spread out

Direct Recall

Circle the letter of the choice that best completes each sentence.

1. Anansi decided to gather together
   a. all the money in the world.   b. all the problems in the world.
   c. all the common sense in the world.

2. Anansi put everything he found
   a. into a large bag.   b. inside a tree.   c. in a big box.

3. Anansi decided to hide what he had found
   a. under a huge rock.   b. at the top of a tree.   c. at the bottom of a tree.

4. Anansi got advice on climbing the tree from
   a. an old man.   b. a small boy.   c. a small girl.

5. In the end, Anansi
   a. kept all the common sense for himself.   b. gave all the common sense to the boy.
   c. threw the common sense into the wind.

Inferential Thinking

Circle the letter of the choice that best completes each item below.

1. Which word best describes Anansi in this story?
   a. greedy
   b. nice
   c. happy

2. Anansi wanted all the common sense in the world so that he could
   a. help other people.
   b. make a lot of money.
   c. do good things.

3. Anansi got very angry because he
   a. really didn't have all the common sense.
   b. thought the boy's advice was bad.
   c. didn't like climbing trees.

4. This folk tale tells how the people of the world
   a. can make mistakes.
   b. have trouble climbing trees.
   c. got common sense.

Critical Thinking

1. Give an example of common sense?

   _____

2. Why do you think common sense is important?

   _____

Vocabulary Development

Using Context Clues to Write Definitions

Read the following paragraph. It is almost the
same as the opening paragraph of the story,
"Getting Common Sense." However, some
words have been added, and some words have
been changed. Use context clues to help you
write a definition for each underlined word.
You can also use your common sense.

One day, Anansi had a brilliant idea. He decided that he would go
around the world and collect all the common sense that there was.
Then, people would need to come to him for assistance whenever
they had problems. Anansi would demand lots of money for his
advice. Soon, he would become very wealthy.

1. brilliant

_____

2. collect

_____

3. assistance

_____

4. demand

_____

5. wealthy

_____

Read the following passage. Then complete the items below by filling in
the correct choices in the answer grid.

> There are many folk tales about Anansi. The stories were first told in
> West Africa. They probably came across the Atlantic Ocean on slave ships.
> Today the Anansi stories are very popular in Jamaica. Anansi is a tricky
> character who often gets into trouble.

1. The Anansi stories were first told
   a. in West Africa.
   b. on the Atlantic Ocean.
   c. in Jamaica.

2. The stories were probably brought across
   the Atlantic Ocean
   a. in books.
   b. by slaves.
   c. by visitors.

3. Anansi is very
   a. tricky.
   b. honest.
   c. caring.

	a	b	c		a	b	c		a	b	c
1.	△	△	△	2.	△	△	△	3.	△	△	△

Applying Your Skills

The reading selection tells how people all over the world got common sense. Write
your own story about how the people in the world got knowledge.

_____

_____

_____

_____

_____

_____

THE MOOSE AND THE COW—
A LOVE STORY

It was October of 1986. It was the mating season for moose in Vermont. There was nothing unusual about that. But then something happened that *was* unusual, very unusual.
- What was going on at Larry Carrara's farm?
- Have you ever heard of a moose who fell in love with a cow?

One day in October 1986, a 700-pound moose wandered onto Larry Carrara's farm in Shrewsbury, Vermont. Although the moose wandered there by accident, it was no accident that he didn't want to leave. The moose had fallen in love!

The object of the moose's love was a brown and white Hereford cow named Jessica. It is impossible for a moose and a cow to mate. But the moose didn't seem to know that. He just stood by Jessica and moaned—in a way that moose moan. He tried to touch her. But Jessica would not have much to do with him.

News of the moose and the cow spread quickly. People started showing up at Larry Carrara's farm to see the moose who was trying to woo a cow. On one Saturday, 4,000 people stopped at the farm. Larry Carrara said his farm was becoming like the World's Fair.

Larry expected the moose to give up on Jessica after about a week or so.

But Larry was wrong. That moose stayed at the farm with Jessica for 76 days. He didn't leave until January of the next year. Animal behavior experts say he left then only because his antlers fell off. When a moose's antlers fall off, its mating season is over for that year.

Larry Carrara was asked why he thought the moose had been so taken with his cow Jessica. "After all," Larry said, "she is very good looking."

mating (MAYT ing)   pairing of animals to produce offspring
woo (WOO)   try to win the love of
behavior (bih HAYV yur)   way of acting
antlers (ANT lurz)   branched horns of animals of the deer family

Direct Recall

Circle the letter of the choice that best completes each sentence.

1. Larry Carrara's farm is in
   a. the World's Fair. **b.** Shrewsbury, Vermont. **c.** Shrewsbury, Virginia.

2. The moose fell in love with a
   a. brown and white Jersey cow. **b.** brown and white Hereford cow.
   c. all brown Hereford cow.

3. Larry Carrara thought the moose would give up on his cow after
   a. a week or so. **b.** a month or so. **c.** 76 days.

4. The moose actually stayed with the cow for
   a. a week or so. **b.** a month or so. **c.** 76 days.

5. Animal behavior experts say the moose finally left the cow because
   a. he got bored. **b.** he was chased away. **c.** his antlers fell off.

Inferential Thinking

Circle the letter of the choice that best completes each item below.

1. You can conclude that the mating season
   for moose starts in the
   a. summer.
   b. fall.
   c. spring.

2. You can conclude that Larry Carrara owned
   a. the moose.
   b. the cow.
   c. the moose and the cow.

3. Which statement is *not* true?
   a. The moose weighed 700 pounds.
   b. In one day, 4,000 people visited the farm.
   c. The moose stayed with Jessica 76 weeks.

4. Another good title for this selection is
   a. "The Odd Couple."
   b. "A Cow."
   c. "A Farm in Vermont."

Critical Thinking

1. Why do you think so many people visited Larry Carrara's farm to see the moose and the cow?

   _____

2. Do you think Larry Carrara could have driven the moose away from his farm? Do you think
   he wanted to? Give reasons for your answers.

   _____

Memory Technique

Using Question Words

You can remember the important facts in a reading selection by asking yourself these questions.

Who?	What?	When?	Where?	Why?

1. *Who* fell in love with a cow named Jessica?

_____

2. *What* did he do after he fell in love?

_____

3. *When* did the story take place?

_____

4. *Where* did the story take place?

_____

5. *Why* was the story unusual?

_____

Test Taking

Read the following passage. Then complete the items below by filling in the correct choices in the answer grid.

> Many animals have special *seasons* when they mate. That is how their *species* stay alive. Usually, of course, animals mate with members of their own species. Once in a while, however, an animal gets *confused* and tries to mate with an animal of a different species—like a certain moose who fell in love with a cow.

1. In this selection, the word *seasons* means
   a. times of year.
   b. flavors.
   c. word.

2. You can conclude that *species* means
   a. colors.
   b. types of animals.
   c. marks.

3. The word *confused* means
   a. sure.
   b. certain.
   c. uncertain.

	a	b	c		a	b	c		a	b	c
1.	△	△	△	2.	△	△	△	3.	△	△	△

Applying Your Skills

Imagine that you were a reporter for a newspaper. Your assignment is to write an article about the moose at Larry Carrara's farm. Write your headline for the news story below.

BLIND SKIERS

Skiing is a sport that takes a lot of skill to master.
- What would it be like to ski if you couldn't see where you were going?
- Have you ever heard of blind people skiing?

Of course, it's very important to know where you're going when you ski. But that doesn't have to stop blind people from enjoying the sport. Blind people can ski with the help of trained guides.

Each blind skier has his or her own sighted guide. The guide skis next to the blind person. The guide describes the trail as the two move along.

"The trail curves to the right here." "You're going to start to go downhill."

It's not easy to become a guide for blind skiers. First of all, a guide must be a good skier. Second, a guide must understand what it's like to ski without being able to see. Skiing blindfolded is part of the training program for the guides. Good guides really serve as the eyes of the blind people they ski with.

Blind skiers enjoy the excitement and freedom of gliding along the snow. Many say they also enjoy the sounds of skiing. They listen for the crunch of the snow under their skis, and the voices of other skiers around them.

Some blind skiers say they enjoy skiing so much they'd like to ski all night. The problem is that when it gets dark, the guides have to stop because they can't see where they're going!

master (MAS tur)   become good at
trained (TRAYND)   taught
sighted (SYT id)   able to see
gliding (GLYD ing)   moving smoothly
crunch (KRUNCH)   crackling sound

Direct Recall

Circle the letter of the choice that best completes each sentence.

1. Blind people
   a. cannot ski.   b. can ski alone.   c. can ski with the help of trained guides.

2. The guides are
   a. sighted.   b. blind.   c. sighted or blind.

3. The guide's job is to
   a. pull the blind skier along.   b. describe the trail.   c. teach skiing.

4. A guide
   a. must be a good skier.   b. does not need to be a good skier.   c. does not need to be trained.

Inferential Thinking

Circle the letter of the choice that best completes each item below.

1. Skiing blindfolded helps the guide
   a. become a faster skier.
   b. understand what it's like to be a blind skier.
   c. learn to ski downhill.

2. Who has the problem skiing at night?
   a. the guides
   b. the blind skiers
   c. neither

3. Who do you think enjoys the excitement of skiing?
   a. only sighted people
   b. only blind people
   c. both sighted and blind people

4. This selection is mainly about
   a. how blind people can ski.
   b. the guide training program.
   c. skiing at night.

Critical Thinking

1. Why do you think a blind person would want to ski?

   _____

2. Why do you think a sighted person would want to become a guide?

   _____

Vocabulary Development

Using Contractions

A *contraction* is a word formed by joining together two words and leaving out one or more letters. An *apostrophe* (') takes the place of the missing letters.

In the selection, you read the following sentences:

Of course, *it's* very important to know where *you're* going when you ski.
But that *doesn't* have to stop blind people from enjoying the sport.

The contraction *it's* stands for the two words *it is*.
The contraction *you're* stands for the two words *you are*.
The contraction *doesn't* stands for the two words *does not*.

Write the contraction that stands for each pair of words below.

1. I am _____

2. were not _____

3. he would _____

4. did not _____

5. she is _____

6. we have _____

7. you will _____

8. they are _____

9. it is _____

10. has not _____

Write the words that each of the following contractions stands for.

11. wasn't _____

12. you'll _____

13. can't _____

14. they've _____

15. wouldn't _____

16. she'll _____

17. we're _____

18. don't _____

19. didn't _____

20. I've _____

Test Taking

Read the following passage. Then complete the items below by filling in the correct choices in the answer grid.

Not too long ago, nobody would have imagined that blind people could ski at all. But many blind people have turned out to be fine skiers. Of course, like sighted skiers, some blind skiers are good and some are not. However, a few blind skiers turned out to be so good that they competed in the Olympics. The 1988 Winter Olympics in Calgary (Canada) had a special event for blind skiers and their guides.

1. Which statement is correct?
   a. All blind skiers are good skiers.
   b. All blind skiers are bad skiers.
   c. Some blind skiers are good skiers, and some are bad skiers.

2. The 1988 Winter Olympics were held in
   a. Lake Placid.
   b. Calgary.
   c. Grenoble.

3. Blind skiers competed in the Olympics
   a. with their guides.
   b. without their guides.
   c. against sighted skiers.

	a	b	c		a	b	c		a	b	c
1.	△	△	△	2.	△	△	△	3.	△	△	△

Applying Your Skills

Unscramble the letters below to form words that were in the story, "Blind Skiers." Then make a word out of the four letters in the circles. That word will tell you what you need in order to go skiing.

1. NLBID   ___ ___ ___ ◯ ___

2. DIGUES   ___ ___ ___ ___ ___ ◯

3. WHILDNOL   ___ ___ ◯ ___ ___ ___ ___ ___

4. FORMEDE   ___ ___ ___ ___ ___ ◯ ___

___ ___ ___ ___

DON'T RIDE THE BUS!

In 1955, when black people wanted to ride a bus in many parts of the South, they had to sit in the back of the bus.
- What happened on December 1, 1955, in Montgomery, Alabama?
- How did a woman named Rosa Parks change history?

Rosa Parks was very tired. She had had a hard day at work. She got on a bus to go home. Mrs. Parks took a seat in the first row of the colored section at the back of the bus.

Soon, all the seats in the white section up front were filled. The bus driver told the black people in the first row of the colored section to get up. They had to give the white people their seats. Everybody got up except Rosa Parks.

The bus driver told Mrs. Parks again that she had to get up. Rosa Parks did not move. She was tired. She had paid her fare. And on that day, she couldn't see why she had to get up to give a white person her seat.

The bus driver left the bus and came back with two policemen. They told Mrs. Parks to get up. Rosa Parks said no. The policemen arrested her.

The next day a big meeting was held in a church in Montgomery. Black people decided that they had been treated unfairly on the buses long enough. They decided to stop riding the buses. They decided that they would all walk to work. Some of them lived so far from their work that they had to get up at 3:00 in the morning. They had to walk for hours. It was a terribly hard thing to do. But they did it. The Montgomery bus boycott lasted 381 days. Black people refused to ride the buses until they gained their rights. The bus company lost thousands and thousands of dollars.

In the end, the Supreme Court ruled that black people could sit anywhere they wanted to on buses. And they would never again have to give up their seats to anybody.

section (SEK shun) part
fare (FAIR) the cost of a ride
treated (TREET id) acted toward
boycott (BOI kot) refusal to buy a product or use a service
Supreme Court (suh PREEM kort) the highest court in the United States

Direct Recall

Circle the letter of the choice that best completes each sentence.

1. Rosa Parks took a seat in the first row of the
   a. colored section at the front of the bus.   b. colored section at the back of the bus.
   c. white section at the front of the bus.

2. After the white section filled up, the bus driver
   a. let white people stand up.   b. did not let anyone else on the bus.
   c. told black people to get up.

3. When Rosa Parks told the policemen she would not get up, they
   a. left her alone.   b. arrested her.   c. tried to make her understand.

4. The next day a big meeting was held
   a. in a church.   b. at the bus company.   c. in a school.

5. In the end, the Supreme Court decided that black people
   a. had to sit in the back of the bus.   b. had to give up their seats to white people.
   c. could sit anywhere they wanted to on buses.

Inferential Thinking

Circle the leter of the choice that best completes each item below.

1. You can conclude that in 1955, in Alabama, when the white section on a bus filled up,
   a. black people always had to get up.
   b. black people could stay in their seats.
   c. the bus driver never said anything.

2. Which word best describes Rosa Parks?
   a. afraid
   b. foolish
   c. brave

3. You can conclude that on other days
   a. Rosa Parks had never given up her seat.
   b. Rosa Parks had given up her seat.
   c. Rosa Parks liked the back of the bus.

4. Another good title for this selection is
   a. "Rosa Parks."
   b. "The Meeting."
   c. "Montgomery, Alabama."

Critical Thinking

1. How do you think people felt when they were told they had to ride in the back of the bus?

_____

2. What was the purpose of the Montgomery bus boycott?

_____

Memory Technique

Making an Outline

Making an outline is a helpful way to remember information. An outline is a list of facts or ideas. Main ideas are written next to a Roman numeral (I, II, III, and so on). Supporting details are listed under the main idea next to a letter (A, B, C, and so on). You do not need to write complete sentences in an outline.

Read the paragraphs below. Then fill in the missing parts of the outline that follows.

There was a meeting of angry people at the Dexter Avenue Baptist Church. They were tired of having to ride at the back of the bus. They were tired of having to give up their seats to white people. And they were furious that Rosa Parks had been arrested.

Together they decided to boycott the buses. First, they said they would not ride the buses on Monday. Then, the boycott grew and grew. People kept walking for 381 days. The leader of the boycott was a man named Martin Luther King, Jr.

I. Meeting of angry people

A. _____

B. _____

C. _____

II. Decided to boycott the buses

A. _____

B. _____

C. _____

D. _____

Test Taking

Read the following passage. Then complete the items below by filling in the correct choices in the answer grid.

> When Rosa Parks was a little girl, she was very excited about starting school. She already knew how to read. Her mother had taught her. Rosa couldn't wait to go to school and learn more. Every day when Rosa went to school, she walked past a big, new school with a lovely yard. That was the school for white children. Rosa's school was a small shack far from her home. It had one room. It had no desks. It hardly had any books. At the age of six, Rosa knew something was not right.

1. When Rosa Parks was a little girl,
   a. she did not want to start school.
   b. she was excited about starting school.
   c. she did not know how to read.

2. In Rosa's town, there was a big, new school
   a. for white children.
   b. for black children.
   c. for all children.

3. How do you think Rosa felt when she first saw her school?
   a. happy
   b. excited
   c. disappointed

	a	b	c		a	b	c		a	b	c
1.	△	△	△	2.	△	△	△	3.	△	△	△

Applying Your Skills

Read the clues below. Then fill in the correct words in the crossword puzzle. All of the answers are in the selection, "Don't Ride the Bus."

Across
2. the highest court in the United States
4. refusal to buy a product or use a service
5. acted toward

Down
1. the cost of a ride
2. part
3. the town where the bus boycott took place

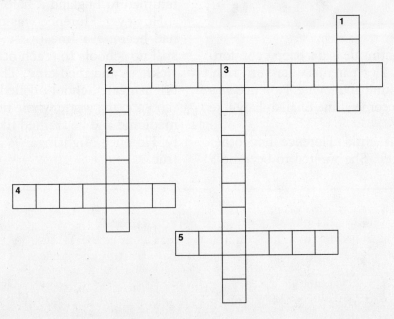

FLORENCE NIGHTINGALE

In the early 1800s, hospitals were unclean places. Nurses were women who couldn't find work anywhere else. They had no training. They helped care for the sick, but they didn't really know anything about medicine.

- Who was Florence Nightingale?
- What did she do to change the nursing profession?

Florence Nightingale had a happy, comfortable childhood. Her parents were very rich. They were also kind and loving. Florence was brought up to become a fine English lady like her mother.

But even as a child, Florence had other dreams for herself. She wanted to become a nurse. She wanted to help people who did not have as much as she did.

Florence told her parents about her dream. They wouldn't hear of it. "Nice girls" did not become nurses in those days. Florence's parents felt that in time she would get rid of her "crazy ideas".

But Florence's crazy ideas stayed with her. She went to a school in Germany to learn to be a nurse. She was taught how to do the things that nurses were supposed to do for patients. But nobody taught her anything about sickness or medicine. There were no nursing schools that taught medicine, so Florence taught herself.

When the Crimean War broke out, Florence Nightingale led a group of women to Turkey to care for the British soldiers. They were the first women ever to work as war nurses. They saved many lives. Florence Nightingale returned to England a hero.

However, Florence was not satisfied. She had become a fine nurse. But there were still no schools to teach other nurses about sickness and medicine. The next year, the Nightingale School opened. It was the first school in the world where nurses could study medicine and be trained like doctors. Finally, Florence Nightingale's dream had come true.

---

training (TRAYN ing)   teaching; education
profession (pruh FESH un)   a job that requires special training
medicine (MED uh sin)   the science of treating and preventing disease
sickness (SIK nis)   the condition of being sick; disease
satisfied (SAT is fyd)   contented; pleased

Direct Recall

Circle the letter of the choice that best completes each sentence.

1. Florence Nightingale's family was
   a. poor. **b.** rich. **c.** not comfortable.

2. As a child, Florence
   a. wanted to become a nurse. **b.** wanted to become a fine lady.
   c. did not know what she wanted to do.

3. At the school in Germany, Florence was
   a. taught about medicine. **b.** not taught about medicine. **c.** not taught anything.

4. When the Crimean War broke out, Florence Nightingale led a group of nurses to
   a. England. **b.** Italy. **c.** Turkey.

5. The Nightingale School was the first in the world where nurses
   a. could go. **b.** did not study medicine. **c.** could study medicine.

Inferential Thinking

Circle the letter of the choice that best completes each item below.

1. Florence's parents did not want her to become a nurse because
   a. "nice girls" did not become nurses.
   b. they did not think she would be a good nurse.
   c. they did not like sick people.

2. In the end, Florence's parents were probably
   a. still sorry she had become a nurse.
   b. proud of her.
   c. angry.

3. Which statement is an opinion?
   a. Florence Nightingale was a nurse.
   b. Florence Nightingale wanted to be a nurse.
   c. Florence Nightingale was an excellent nurse.

4. Another good title for this selection is
   a. "The Woman Who Changed Nursing."
   b. "A School in Germany."
   c. "War Nurses."

Critical Thinking

1. Why do you think Florence Nightingale was not satisfied with becoming a "fine English lady?"

2. Florence Nightingale's parents expected her to grow up in a certain way. She had different plans for herself. Do you think it is hard to go against your parents' wishes? Give reasons for your answer.

Understanding Prefixes

A *prefix* is a group of letters put before the beginning of a word to make a new word.

In the selection "Florence Nightingale," you read the word *unclean*. The word *unclean* has the prefix *un-*. The prefix *un-* means "not." The word *unclean* means "not clean."

Combine the prefix *un-* with the words below to make new words. Then write the meaning of each new word.

	New Word	Meaning
1. *un-* + happy		
2. *un-* + kind		
3. *un-* + sure		
4. *un-* + healthy		
5. *un-* + important		

Now write a sentence for each new word. Make sure your sentence shows that you understand the meaning of the new word.

6. _____

7. _____

8. _____

9. _____

10. _____

Test Taking

Read the following passage. Then complete the items below by filling in the correct choices in the answer grid.

Even as a little girl, Florence Nightingale wanted to be a nurse. She loved to play hospital with her dolls. She put bandages and splints on them all the time. Once, Florence actually saved the life of a neighbor's dog. As she got a little older, Florence helped take care of sick people in her village. Florence was a child who always knew what she wanted to do when she grew up.

1. The main idea of this passage is that Florence Nightingale
   a. always knew what she wanted to do when she grew up.
   b. liked to play hospital with her dolls.
   c. helped care for sick people in her village.

2. Florence once saved the life of
   a. her sister's dog.
   b. her neighbor's dog.
   c. her neighbor's cat.

3. Which statement is *not* true?
   a. Florence put bandages on her dolls.
   b. Florence helped care for sick people.
   c. Florence did not want to be a nurse.

	a	b	c		a	b	c		a	b	c
1.	△	△	△	2.	△	△	△	3.	△	△	△

Applying Your Skills

Imagine that this ad was printed in an English newspaper in the year 1800. Use the information that you have read to tell what is not right about the ad.

Help Wanted

Trained nurses to work in clean, downtown hospital

_____

_____

_____

_____

SPUTNIK

Before 1957, the world of space travel existed only in books and in people's imaginations.
- What happened in 1957?
- What was Sputnik?

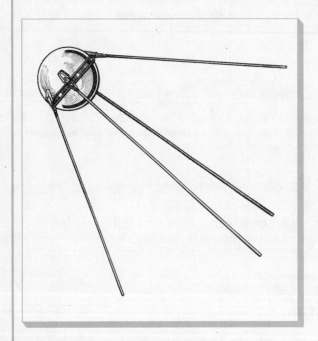

On October 4, 1957, the Soviet Union launched the first human-made satellite. It was called *Sputnik*. *Sputnik* is a Russian word that means traveler. The satellite traveled in an orbit around the earth every 95 minutes. It went at a speed of 18,000 miles each hour. The launch of *Sputnik* marked the beginning of the space age. It also marked the beginning of the space race.

Many people in the United States were upset that the Soviet Union had sent up the first satellite. They wanted to know why Americans didn't have satellites. Then, on November 3, 1957, the Russians sent up *Sputnik 2*. There was a live dog inside the satellite. People in the United States became even more upset. The space race was really on.

Less than three months later, the United States launched its first satellite. It was called *Explorer 1*.

The following summer, the United States created the National Aeronautics and Space Administration. You know it better as NASA. NASA's job was to plan the country's space trips.

For more than 30 years, the United States and the Soviet Union have kept sending satellites into space. The space age goes on. The space race goes on, too.

imaginations (ih maj uh NAY shunz)   power of forming pictures in the mind
launched (LAUNCHT)   pushed off
satellite (SAT ul yt)   an object that goes around a body in space
orbit (OR bit)   the path followed by a satellite; a single trip by a satellite around a body in space
created (kree AY tid)   brought into being; made

Direct Recall

Circle the letter of the choice that best completes each sentence.

1. The first human-made satellite was called
   a. *Sputnik.*   **b.** *Sputnik 2.*   **c.** *Explorer 1.*

2. The first satellite traveled in an orbit around the earth every
   a. 4 minutes.   **b.** 95 minutes.   **c.** 180 minutes.

3. Many Americans were upset because
   a. the Soviet Union had no satellites.
   b. the Soviet Union had sent up the first satellite.
   c. the United States had sent up the first satellite.

4. *Explorer 1* was
   a. the first human-made satellite.   **b.** the second Russian satellite.
   c. the first United States satellite.

5. NASA's job is to
   a. plan space trips.   **b.** plan airplane trips.   **c.** launch *Sputnik.*

Inferential Thinking

Circle the letter of the choice that best completes each item below.

1. How many satellites did the Soviet Union launch before the United States lauched one?
   a. one
   b. two
   c. three

2. You can conclude that people in the Soviet Union are called
   a. Russians.
   b. Unions.
   c. Americans.

3. The popular name for the National Aeronautics and Space Administration was formed by
   a. making the first word shorter.
   b. combining the first letters of each main word.
   c. combining the last letters of each main word.

4. Another good title for this selection is
   a. "*Explorer 1.*"
   b. "Fast Travel."
   c. "The Beginning of the Space Race."

Critical Thinking

1. Why do you think people want to explore space?

   _____

2. Why do you think people cared which country sent up the first satellite?

   _____

Memory Technique

Learning Spelling Words

Lots of people have trouble remembering how words are spelled. Try using the method below to learn how to spell the vocabulary words at the bottom of page 110.

1. Look at the word carefully.
2. Say it out loud.
3. Close your eyes and picture the word in your mind.
4. Look at the word again, and make sure your picture of it was correct.
5. Now, write the word from memory in the column below labeled "First Try."
6. Check to see if you spelled the word correctly. If you made a mistake, redo steps 1 through 4. Then try to write the word again in the column labeled "Second Try."
7. Now go on to the next vocabulary word.

	First Try	Second Try
1.	_____	_____
2.	_____	_____
3.	_____	_____
4.	_____	_____
5.	_____	_____

Test Taking

Look at the following chart. Then complete the items below by filling in the correct choices in the answer grid.

EARLY SPACE FLIGHTS

Spacecraft	Country	Date Launched	Importance
Sputnick 1	Soviet Union	Oct. 4, 1957	first human-made satellite
Sputnick 2	Soviet Union	Nov. 3, 1957	first satellite to carry a live being (a dog)
Explorer 1	United States	Feb. 1, 1958	first United States satellite

1. *Sputnik 1* was launched on
   a. Oct. 4, 1957.
   b. Nov. 3, 1957.
   c. Feb. 1, 1958.

2. The first United States satellite was called
   a. *Sputnik 1.*
   b. *Sputnik 2.*
   c. *Explorer 1.*

3. A dog was aboard
   a. *Sputnik 1.*
   b. *Sputnik 2.*
   c. *Explorer 1.*

	a	b	c		a	b	c		a	b	c
1.	△	△	△	2.	△	△	△	3.	△	△	△

Applying Your Skills

This is a picture of the first human-made satellite. Make up your own design for a satellite. Draw it in the box.

IT COULD ALWAYS BE WORSE

People say you shouldn't complain because things could be worse. This story from Jewish folklore tells how things could get worse—and did.

- What was the poor farmer's problem?
- How did the rabbi help the farmer to be happy with what he had?

The poor farmer couldn't stand it anymore. He went to the rabbi to get help.

"Rabbi," he said. "What can I do? My house is so crowded. I live with my wife, my six children, and my in-laws. All we have is a one-room hut. Everybody is fighting all the time. We must have more room."

The rabbi thought. Then he said, "Do not worry, my son. Just promise to do exactly what I tell you. Everything will be fine."

"I promise," said the farmer.

The rabbi asked the farmer what animals he owned. The farmer said he had a cow, a goat, and some chickens. The rabbi told the farmer to go home and put all the animals in the house. The farmer thought the rabbi was crazy. But he had promised to do exactly what the rabbi told him. So he did.

The next day, the farmer ran to the rabbi and said, "Things are not better. They're worse. My house is like a barn."

The rabbi told the farmer to take the chickens out of the house. The next day, the farmer ran to the rabbi again. He said the goat was smashing everything in the house. The rabbi said to take the goat out of the house. The next day, the farmer told the rabbi nobody could stand to live with the cow another minute. The rabbi said to take the cow out of the house.

The following day, the farmer ran to the rabbi one last time. "Thank you," he said. "Everything is fine now. Without the animals, the house is clean and quiet. And we all have plenty of room."

complain (kum PLAYN)   say that something is wrong; to find fault
rabbi (RAB eye)   a teacher or leader in the Jewish religion
in-laws (IN lawz)   relatives by marriage; family of one's husband or wife
hut (HUT)   small, plain dwelling
exactly (ig ZAKT lee)   precisely; just the same as

Direct Recall

Circle the letter of the choice that best completes each sentence.

1. The poor farmer went to the rabbi
   a. to pray.   b. to get help.   c. to visit.

2. The farmer's house was too
   a. ugly.   b. large.   c. crowded.

3. The rabbi said the farmer should promise to
   a. do exactly what he told him.   b. move to another house.   c. fill his house with animals.

4. The rabbi told the farmer to put his animals
   a. in the barn.   b. in the house.   c. in the basement.

5. At the end of the story, the farmer said
   a. the house was still too crowded.   b. everybody was fighting.   c. they had plenty of room.

Inferential Thinking

Circle the letter of the choice that best completes each item below.

1. Which word best describes the farmer at the beginning of the story?
   a. upset
   b. happy
   c. funny

2. Which word best describes the farmer at the end of the story?
   a. upset
   b. happy
   c. funny

3. Which word best describes the rabbi?
   a. stupid
   b. sad
   c. clever

4. The farmer did what the rabbi told him because he
   a. thought the rabbi had a good idea.
   b. thought the rabbi was crazy.
   c. had promised to do what the rabbi said.

Critical Thinking

1. Why did the farmer think everything was fine at the end of the story?

_____

2. How does this story tell you to help yourself be happy with what you have?

_____

Vocabulary Development

Understanding Suffixes

In the selection "It Could Always Be Worse," you read the word *farmer*. The word *farmer* has the suffix *-er*. A *suffix* is one or more letters added to the end of a word to make a new word. The suffix *-er* means "a person who." *Farmer* means "a person who farms."

Combine the following words with the suffix *-er* to make new words. Then write the meanings of the new words. Check a dictionary if you need help.

	New Word	**Meaning**
1. sing	_____	_____
2. teach	_____	_____
3. camp	_____	_____
4. build	_____	_____
5. catch	_____	_____

Now write a sentence using each new word you made. Make sure your sentences show that you understand the meanings of the new words.

6. _____

7. _____

8. _____

9. _____

10. _____

Test Taking

Look at the following dictionary entry. Then, complete the items below by filling in the correct choices in the answer grid.

folklore (FOHK lor)   stories, beliefs, and customs of a people, handed down from generation to generation

1. The word *folklore* has
   a. one syllable.
   b. two syllables.
   c. three syllables.

2. The accent is on the
   a. first syllable.
   b. second syllable.
   c. third syllable.

3. The word *folklore* is
   a. a noun.
   b. a verb.
   c. an adjective.

	a	b	c		a	b	c		a	b	c
1.	△	△	△	2.	△	△	△	3.	△	△	△

Applying Your Skills

Look at the cartoon below. Explain why the farmer at the end looks different from the way he looked at the beginning.

_____

_____

_____

_____

_____

_____

THE MYSTERY OF THE DINOSAUR

More than 200 million years ago, dinosaurs appeared on the earth. About 65 million years ago, they disappeared.
- What happened to make the dinosaur die out?
- Will anybody ever really know?

Dinosaurs were the largest animals ever to live on land. For 140 million years, they ruled the animal world. Then, the dinosaurs all died out. There are many theories that attempt to explain what caused the dinosaurs to die out.

One theory is that during the time of the dinosaurs, the weather on earth suddenly became much, much colder. Dinosaurs had no fur or feathers to protect them from the cold. They were too large to hide in warm places. So they died.

Another weather theory has it that an asteroid crashed into the earth. Dust from the crash blocked the light and the heat given off by the sun. Again, the weather became too cold for the dinosaurs.

Some scientists believe that a star blew up during the lifetime of the dinosaurs. The explosion may have produced dangerous radiation. The radiation could have killed the dinosaurs.

Other scientists believe that the dinosaurs' problems had to do with food. Some dinosaurs ate nothing but plants. The plants that the dinosaurs ate stopped growing. New plants appeared, but they were not good for the dinosaurs. So, the plant-eating dinosaurs had no food. And they died off.

The meat-eating dinosaurs had a different food problem. Many new kinds of animals began to appear in the places where the dinosaurs lived. They were smaller than dinosaurs, so they could move more quickly. That made them better able to catch the prey that they and the meat-eating dinosaurs needed for food. So, the meat-eating dinosaurs also had no food. And they died off.

There is probably no single theory that explains why the dinosaurs died out. We do know that conditions on the earth changed during their lifetime. And the dinosaurs could not change with them.

theories (THEE uh reez)   explanations of how or why something happens
asteroid (AS tuh roid)   small rocky body that revolves around the sun
radiation (ray dee AY shun)   energy given off in the form of rays
prey (PRAY)   an animal hunted for food by another animal
single (SING gul)   only one
conditions (kin DISH unz)   the way things are

Direct Recall

Circle the letter of the choice that best completes each sentence.

1. Dinosaurs ruled the animal world for
   a. 65 million years.   **b.** 140 million years.   **c.** 200 million years.

2. Dinosaurs had
   a. fur and feathers.   **b.** fur, but no feathers.   **c.** no fur or feathers.

3. One theory is that a star
   a. crashed into the earth.   **b.** came close to the earth.   **c.** blew up and gave off radiation.

4. Another theory says that dust from an asteroid crash may have blocked light and heat of
   a. the sun.   **b.** the earth.   **c.** the moon.

5. Another theory says that plant-eating dinosaurs could not eat
   a. new animals that appeared on the earth.   **b.** new plants that appeared on the earth.
   c. asteroids that crashed into the earth.

Inferential Thinking

Circle the letter of the choice that best completes each item below.

1. Dinosaurs may have died out because
   a. they had no fur or feathers.
   b. they ruled for 140 million years.
   c. some dinosaurs didn't need food.

2. You can conclude that
   a. all dinosaurs ate only plants.
   b. all dinosaurs ate only meat.
   c. some dinosaurs ate plants, and some ate meat.

3. All of the theories about the end of the dinosaurs have to do with
   a. stars blowing up.
   b. changing conditions on the earth.
   c. new animals appearing on the earth.

4. Which statement is *not* true?
   a. Scientists know exactly why dinosaurs died out.
   b. Dinosaurs were the largest animals on land.
   c. Dinosaurs died out 65 million years ago.

Critical Thinking

1. Why do you think there are so many different theories about why dinosaurs died out?

   _____

2. Why do you think scientists want to know why dinosaurs died out?

   _____

Writing Summaries

A useful way to remember information from a reading selection is to write a summary. A *summary* is a short statement of the important ideas in a selection.

You just read about five different theories of how the dinosaur died out. In your own words, summarize each theory. Write one or two sentences for each. You may look back at the selection if you need help.

Colder Weather

_____

_____

_____

_____

_____

_____

_____

Asteroid Crash

_____

_____

_____

_____

_____

_____

_____

Star Blown Up

_____

_____

_____

_____

_____

_____

_____

New Plants

_____

_____

_____

_____

_____

_____

_____

New Animals

_____

_____

_____

_____

_____

_____

_____

Test Taking

Read the following passage. Then complete the items below by filling in the correct choices in the answer grid.

Before the 1800s, nobody knew that dinosaurs had ever lived on the earth. In 1822, a woman in England found a very large tooth buried in a rock. Then, bones and teeth from several other very large animals were found. In 1841, a scientist named Sir Richard Owen said he thought these teeth and bones were from animals that were not like any animals people had ever seen. He named them dinosaurs. The word means "terrible lizards." Dinosaurs were not really lizards. But their size would certainly have made them seem terrible.

1. People did not know anything about dinosaurs
   a. before the 1800s.
   b. after the 1800s.
   c. before the 1900s.

2. A woman in England found a
   a. skeleton buried in a rock.
   b. tooth buried in a rock.
   c. large bone buried in a rock.

3. Dinosaurs were named by
   a. a woman in England.
   b. Sir Richard Owen.
   c. a terrible lizard.

	a	b	c		a	b	c		a	b	c
1.	△	△	△	2.	△	△	△	3.	△	△	△

Applying Your Skills

Make up your own theory about what happened to make the dinosaurs die out. Write it in the space below.

_____

_____

_____

_____

_____

_____

THE WANDERING WHALE

Imagine you are a farmer. You are looking out at your fields one day, and a whale swims by.
- Have you ever heard of Humphrey the Humpback Whale?
- How could a whale swim almost halfway across California?

Farmers, ranchers, and children watched in amazement one day as a 40-foot, 45-ton humpback whale swam up the Sacramento River into the farmlands of California. It was quite a sight. The whale had probably been on its way south along the coastline from Alaska and made a wrong turn.

As the whale swam farther upstream, a serious problem developed. Whales are used to living in salt water and cannot exist for a long time in fresh water. Marine biologists who were keeping track of the whale's progress upstream tried to think of a way to make it turn around and go back to the ocean. They played recorded sounds of unfriendly whales upstream to try to frighten the humpback whale. They played sounds of friendly whales downstream to lure it in that direction. The whale was not interested. It kept swimming the wrong way.

Hundreds of people lined up to see this amazing animal. They decided it was probably a male and they called him Humphrey. The marine biologists were afraid Humphrey would be too weak to return to the ocean if they couldn't turn him around soon. They would get him going in the right direction for a while. Then, he would swim back upstream. Soon, the newspapers started calling him "Humphrey the Wrong-Way Whale."

After several weeks, Humphrey began to swim in the right direction. But he was very weak. And another problem had developed. To reach the sea, Humphrey had to swim under many bridges. The traffic on the bridges made him very nervous. To help Humphrey, traffic was stopped whenever he had to swim under a bridge.

Finally, only one bridge was left. Thousands of people came out to watch. When Humphrey got close to the last bridge, everybody looked on silently. Then, Humphrey did a tremendous backflip and, as thousands cheered, he swam under the Golden Gate Bridge and headed out to his ocean home.

amazement (uh MAYZ munt) great surprise
upstream (UP streem) in a direction or place toward the higher part of a stream or river
marine biologists (muh REEN by OL uh jists) scientists who study sea plants and animals
downstream (DOUN streem) in a direction or place toward the lower part of a stream or river
silently (SY lunt lee) without making a sound
tremendous (trih MEN dus) very, very big

Direct Recall

Circle the letter of the choice that best completes each sentence.

1. Humphrey was probably swimming south from
   a. Alaska.   b. Mexico.   c. The United States.

2. A whale cannot
   a. eat river food.   b. live long in fresh water.   c. swim downstream.

3. Humphrey kept swimming
   a. away from the ocean.   b. toward the ocean.   c. too fast to catch.

4. The traffic on bridges made Humphrey
   a. excited.   b. happy.   c. nervous.

5. Before Humphrey went out to sea, he
   a. got lost.   b. did a tremendous backflip.   c. tipped over a boat.

Inferential Thinking

Circle the letter of the choice that best completes each item below.

1. The newspapers called him "Humphrey the Wrong-Way Whale" because he
   a. stopped traffic on the bridges.
   b. was going away from the ocean.
   c. was swimming backwards.

2. You can conclude that salt water is
   a. necessary for whales.
   b. harmful to whales.
   c. not important.

3. If marine biologists had not turned Humphrey around, he would have
   a. not had enough food.
   b. kept swimming.
   c. died.

4. The whale was probably
   a. confused.
   b. angry.
   c. shy.

Critical Thinking

1. Why do you think so many people cared about Humphrey?

   _____

2. Do you think Humphrey knew that people were trying to help him? Explain your answer.

   _____

Vocabulary Development

Forming Compound Words

In the selection, you read the words *upstream* and *downstream*. These are compound words. Compound words are made by joining two words to make a new word. The word *upstream* is made by joining the words *up* and *stream*. *Downstream* is made by joining the words *down* and *stream*.

Read the words below. Draw a line between a word in column A that can join a word in column B to make a new word.

A	B
farm	line
coast	body
back	water
every	paper
sun	shine
half	land
news	time
night	way
under	flip

Write your new words below.

_____

_____

_____

Test Taking

Read the following passage. Then complete the items below by filling in the correct choices in the answer grid.

Humpback whales live in all the oceans and often swim in waters near coastlines. They grow no larger than 40 to 50 feet in length and look rather chubby. The humpback whale has bumps on its head and long flippers. Its body is black on top and white underneath.

1. You can conclude that Humphrey was near California because humpback whales
   a. often swim near coastlines.
   b. have long flippers.
   c. are black on top and white underneath.

2. Humpback whales grow no longer than
   a. 30 feet.
   b. 50 feet.
   c. 75 feet.

3. You can conclude that Humphrey was
   a. bigger than most whales.
   b. just a baby whale.
   c. an average-sized humpback whale.

	a	b	c		a	b	c		a	b	c
1.	△	△	△	2.	△	△	△	3.	△	△	△

Applying Your Skills

Many people had ideas about helping Humphrey. Some of them wrote letters to the newspapers. Some of these ideas were silly. Some ideas were good.

Write a make-believe letter to someone who could help Humphrey. Tell them how you would turn a 40-foot whale around.

_____

_____

_____

_____

_____

_____

_____

_____

_____

_____

_____

A HISTORY OF FIRE

Suppose you wanted to cook hot dogs over a campfire. Here's what you would do. First, you would gather small pieces of wood. Then, you would take a match and light the fire. Simple, isnt' it?

- How could you start a campfire without using matches?
- When do you think matches were invented?

Long ago, people did not know how to make fire. Probably they found fires that had been started accidentally—by lightning or by the flames shooting out of volcanoes. When people first found fire, they soon learned to use it. Fire gave them heat and light. It protected them from wild animals. It made it possible for them to cook their food. Since they did not know how to make fire, they had to carry it around with them from place to place.

Later, people did learn how to make fire. They discovered that they could produce a spark if they struck two hard stones against each other. When they got the spark, they carefully fed it with dried leaves or small pieces of wood. Suddenly, they would have fire. Another way ancient people made fire was by rubbing two sticks together. Both of these ways to make fire worked, but both were very slow and difficult.

It wasn't until much, much later that fire-making became easy. It happened less than 200 years ago, in 1836, with the invention of wooden matches with phosphorus tips. The trouble then was that it was not only easy to make fires, it was too easy. The phosphorus-tipped match was very dangerous because it could be lit from almost any surface. Also, the phosphorus was unhealthy to handle. It could make people ill.

These problems were not solved until the invention of the safety match. The "safety" of this match is based upon a simple idea. A chemical that can produce fire is put on the tip of each match. Another chemical is put on a special section of the ouside of the container in which safety matches are kept. A safety match can produce fire only when its tip is struck against this special section.

After thousands of years, the search is over. People have a way to make fire that is not only easy but also safe.

---

campfire (KAMP fyr) an outdoor fire, as at a campsite
lightning (LYT ning) a flash of light in the sky caused by electricity passing between clouds or between a cloud and the earth
phosphorus (FOS fur us) a chemical that can make fire
unhealthy (un HEL thee) not good for living things
chemical (KEM ih kul) a substance that can produce an effect by itself or in combination with another substance
invention (in VEN shun) the act of thinking out or making something that did not exist before

Direct Recall

Circle the letter of the choice that best completes each sentence.

1. People in early times found fires started by
   a. animals.   **b.** lightning or volcanoes.   **c.** matches.

2. Hundreds of years ago, people did not make fires with
   a. matches.   **b.** sticks.   **c.** stones.

3. Fires were slow and difficult to
   a. start.   **b.** put out.   **c.** control.

4. The problem with phosphorus was that it was
   a. dangerous.   **b.** hard to make.   **c.** expensive.

5. The safety match ended a search that lasted for
   a. a century.   **b.** thousands of years.   **c.** ten years.

Inferential Thinking

Circle the letter of the choice that best completes each item below.

1. In early times, wild animals were probably
   a. not afraid of fire.
   b. afraid of fire.
   c. afraid of people.

2. Before matches were invented, fire-making tools were
   a. hard to carry.
   b. easy to make.
   c. never used.

3. Early matches
   a. caused many accidents.
   b. were hard to carry.
   c. were not made of wood.

4. A good title for this selection is
   a. "Fire from Volcanoes."
   b. "Why Fire is Important."
   c. "The Story of Fire."

Critical Thinking

1. Why was the invention of matches so important to people? Give reasons for your answer.

_____

2. Why do you think people like sitting around a campfire?

_____

Organizing Information

It is hard to remember things that are not put together in any special way.

A good way to remember the order in which things happen is to list them in that order. Sometimes there are cue words such as: *first*, *next*, *then*, *later*, and *last* in a story. These words will help you put events in order.

Read "A History of Fire" again. List the main idea of each paragraph on the lines below. Use the cue words to help you.

1. Long, long ago, _____

2. Later, _____

3. Much, much later, _____

4. Last, _____

Test Taking

Read the following passage. Then, complete the items below by filling in the correct choices in the answer grid.

Some early people used wooden "drills" to make fire. They wound a string around a stick and put the stick on a flat piece of wood. One person held the stick straight up. Then two others pulled on the string, first one way and then the other way. They could make fire fairly quickly, but three people were needed to do it.

1. An early tool for making fire worked like a
   a. hammer.
   b. drill.
   c. ruler.

2. This way of making fire was
   a. quick.
   b. very hard.
   c. took a long time.

3. A problem in making fire this way was that
   a. three people were needed.
   b. it was cold outside.
   c. they had no sticks.

	a	b	c		a	b	c		a	b	c
1.	△	△	△	2.	△	△	△	3.	△	△	△

Applying Your Skills

Suppose you were a person living long ago. You find fire. You have never seen fire before.

Write a paragraph telling how you would feel and what you would do.

_____

_____

_____

_____

_____

A SILENT CLOWN

The job of a comedian is to make people laugh.
- Do you think you would like to be a comedian?
- How could you make people laugh without speaking?

Harpo Marx spent fifty years of his life working in vaudeville and in the movies. He and his brothers made up one of the most famous comedy teams in history—the Marx Brothers. Strangely, Harpo didn't start out wanting to be a comedian. When he was a young man, Harpo wanted to play baseball for the New York Giants.

Harpo became a stage performer for a very strange reason. Harpo's family was very poor. His mother naturally wanted her children to be rich. She decided that her four sons could become rich and famous if they went into show business.

One day when he was fourteen, Harpo was playing the piano in a movie theater. His mother came in and rushed him outside. She told him that he and his brothers had to sing on stage in one hour. Harpo was terrified. He was so frightened, in fact, that when he and his brothers stood in front of the audience, Harpo just stood there and stared. He didn't sing a note!

The "singing" Marx Brothers act traveled all around the United States. Slowly, the brothers discovered that people liked them better when they were being silly and funny than when they were trying to be singers.

One day, someone told Harpo that he was funniest when he was silent. For the rest of his years as a performer, Harpo never spoke a word. Many people thought that there was something wrong with his voice, but there wasn't. Harpo had a fine voice. He was just funnier being a silent clown than a vocal one.

Harpo Marx performed for many years. Even though he hated doing it at first, he came to love it. Harpo Marx, who once had to be pushed onto the stage, became one of the world's great silent clowns.

comedian (kuh MEE dee un)   an actor who plays comic parts
vaudeville (VAWD vil)   a stage show with songs, dances, and comic acts
performer (pur FAWRM ur)   a person who entertains on stage in front of an audience
terrified (TER uh fyd)   very frightened
audience (AW dee uns)   people gathered to hear or watch something, such as a vaudeville act, a movie, or a play

Direct Recall

Circle the letter of the choice that best completes each sentence.

1. Harpo Marx really wanted to be a
   a. baseball player. b. comedian. c. piano player.

2. He went on the stage with his brothers when he was
   a. sixty-nine years old. b. fourteen years old. c. six years old.

3. When he first went on stage he was
   a. excited. b. terrified. c. bored.

4. People liked the Marx Brothers best when they
   a. sang. b. danced. c. were silly and funny.

5. Many people thought that something was wrong with Harpo's
   a. voice. b. ears c. car.

Inferential Thinking

Circle the letter of the choice that best completes each item below.

1. You can conclude that Harpo never got to be
   a. a comedian.
   b. a baseball player.
   c. famous.

2. You can infer that Harpo's mother was very
   a. shy.
   b. uncertain.
   c. forceful.

3. Harpo didnt' speak
   a. on stage.
   b. anywhere.
   c. to his brothers.

4. Which statement is not true?
   a. Harpo wanted to be a baseball player.
   b. Harpo couldn't speak.
   c. Harpo was a silent clown.

Critical Thinking

1. Do you think it is good for people to perform in front of an audience if they are frightened? Why or why not?

   _____

2. Name three qualities that you think make someone funny.

   _____

Vocabulary Development

Using Context Clues

Sometimes you can figure out what a word means by looking at the words around it. Only certain words will make sense in that place in the sentence.

In the story "A Silent Clown," the word *audience* clearly means people watching a show.

Read the sentences below. Circle the letter of the choice that best tells the meaning of the underlined word.

1. People laughed at the Marx Brothers' <u>vaudeville</u> shows.
   a. art.   **b.** sports.   **c.** comedy.

2. As a <u>performer</u>, Harpo made many people happy.
   a. entertainer.   **b.** fighter.   **c.** brother.

3. If shy people were forced to be on stage, they would be <u>terrified</u>.
   a. happy.   **b.** pleased.   **c.** frightened.

4. A <u>comedian's</u> job is to make people laugh.
   a. piano player's.   **b.** performer's.   **c.** comic actor's.

Test Taking

Read the following passage. Then complete the items below by filling in the correct choices in the answer grid.

> One day, the mother of the Marx Brothers decided that her sons' act needed something extra. She sent a package to her son Arthur. He thought that it might be a new costume, but it was a harp. Arthur didn't know how to play the harp, but he taught himself. For the rest of his life, no one called him Arthur. They called him Harpo.

1. Arthur's mother sent him a package because
   a. she thought her sons' act needed something extra.
   b. it was his birthday.
   c. she wanted to change his name.

2. He learned to play the harp
   a. from a fine teacher.
   b. by himself.
   c. from his brothers.

3. A good title for this passage is
   a. "Minnie Marx's Son."
   b. "How Harpo Got His Name."
   c. "The Marx Brothers' Vaudeville Act."

	a	b	c		a	b	c		a	b	c
1.	△	△	△	2.	△	△	△	3.	△	△	△

Applying Your Skills

Write a short plot for a movie starring Harpo Marx. Remember that he is funny, he doesn't speak, and he plays the harp.

_____

_____

_____

_____

_____

_____

_____

_____

_____

_____

_____

PASS THE NAPKIN

People don't usually think about napkins. However, someone had to invent napkins. There had to be a reason to do this.

- Why do you think napkins were invented?
- What do you think people did before there were napkins?

Long ago, when kings and queens had a special feast, all the guests would sit at a long table. The table would be covered with a fancy tablecloth. Tablecloths were made by hand then and were very expensive. In fact, tablecloths were so expensive that even kings and queens had only one.

In those early days, people didn't use knives and forks when they ate. They ate with their hands. When they finished eating, they would wipe their fingers and mouths on the tablecloth. What a mess! You can imagine that after several feasts a tablecloth would be ruined. So, the king and queen would have to have a new one made.

Years later, someone had a bright idea. They put a *little* tablecloth over the *big* one at the place where the king and queen sat. And each guest at the feast was given a small towel. After everyone was finished eating, a servant would bring a basin of water to the king and queen. They dipped their hands in the water and then wiped them on the little tablecloth. The guests all dipped their hands into water basins, too. Then, they dried their hands on the small towels. The little tablecloths and small towels were the first napkins.

After a time, it became the custom to put a fancy white napkin on the table at each guest's place. But the servants would bring in towels, anyway. That way, the guests could use the towels, and the beautiful napkins wouldn't get dirty!

In a way, people do almost the same thing today. Many people have pretty napkins that they use only when they have guests. They have less fancy ones or paper napkins for everyday use. When you use paper napkins today, you are just like the kings and queens of long ago. You are keeping your fancy napkins clean!

---

feast (FEEST)   a large, fancy meal
expensive (ik SPEN siv)   having a high price; costing a lot
servant (SUR vunt)   a person who works in someone else's home
basin (BAYS un)   a round, shallow bowl for holding liquids
custom (KUS tum)   a usual way of doing things

Direct Recall

Circle the letter of the choice that best completes each sentence.

1. Long ago, tablecloths were
   a. expensive.   **b.** small.   **c.** easy to buy.

2. Even kings and queens had
   a. many tablecloths.   **b.** only white tablecloths.   **c.** only one tablecloth.

3. People used tablecloths to
   a. wipe the silverware.   **b.** wipe their hands and mouths.   **c.** dip into the water basins.

4. After several feasts, a tablecloth would be
   a. ruined.   **b.** decorated.   **c.** fancy.

5. In those days, people
   a. ate with their hands.   **b.** all had servants.   **c.** brought their own napkins.

Inferential Thinking

1. Napkins were invented
   a. after silverware.
   b. to save tablecloths.
   c. because servants were hard to get.

2. You can conclude that people long ago probably
   a. didn't have laundries.
   b. were very neat.
   c. didn't like knives and forks.

3. After knives and forks began to be used, people
   a. stopped using napkins.
   b. used fancier tablecloths.
   c. kept using napkins.

4. Another good title for this story is
   a. "The King's Servants."
   b. "Where Napkins Came From."
   c. "Why Napkins Were Invented."

Critical Thinking

1. What might a person of long ago think of the way people eat today? Give reasons for your answer.

   _____

2. If you could have only one tool to eat with, which one would you choose? Give reasons for your answer.

   _____

Picturing Details

Suppose you wanted to remember a list of items. Here is one way to do it:

1. Read the list.
2. Picture in your mind how each item looks.
3. Think about where it might go.

Practice: Use the words in the list to label each item.

mug

napkin

plate

tablecloth

knife

basin

Now test yourself. Cover the picture and the list. Think about the table setting you made. Write a list telling what was on the table.

_____   _____

_____   _____

_____   _____

Test Taking

Read the following passage. Then complete the items below by filling in the correct choices in the answer grid.

> Forks are very old tools. They were used for many different things, but no one thought of using them to eat with. In the 16th century, people in Italy began eating with forks. People in England thought this was a big joke. They made fun of people who were afraid to get their fingers dirty. By the end of the 17th century, however, most people were eating with forks.

1. Before the 17th century, most English people probably ate with
   a. forks.
   b. their hands.
   c. silver spoons.

2. In England, they thought people who used forks were
   a. too fussy.
   b. weak.
   c. rich.

3. A good title for this article is
   a. "Why People Use Forks."
   b. "A Tool for Eating."
   c. "How to Hold a Fork."

	a	b	c		a	b	c		a	b	c
1.	△	△	△	2.	△	△	△	3.	△	△	△

Applying Your Skills

Read the cartoon. How *do* people get information about long-ago times? Write what you think.

_____

_____

_____

THE HEAVENLY ARCHER

Do you ever look at the sun and wonder about it? How and why does it cross the sky? Many people tell stories to explain things in nature. This story comes from China and is very old.

- What does this story explain?
- Who was the Heavenly Archer?

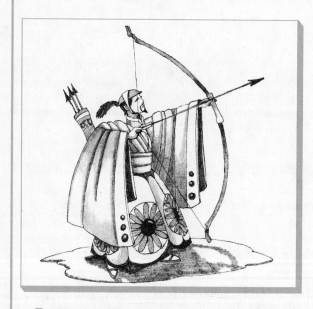

Long, long ago, there was a wise emperor named Yao. His people were happy and lived in peace.

At that time, at the edge of the world, there was a certain tree. In its branches were ten suns. Each day, one sun would cross the sky and light the world.

One day, all ten suns decided to cross the sky together. As the ten suns rose, the world became so hot that plants and animals died. The people shut themselves in their houses and trembled. When evening came, they went to the wise emperor.

"Help us," they said. "The earth cannot stand another day like this." Emperor Yao asked that the Heavenly Archer be sent down to earth. Shen, the Heavenly Archer, was the greatest archer in the world.

Emperor Yao and Shen had a plan. They sat together and waited for the dawn. Shen had his bow ready and there were ten arrows in his quiver. Soon, the suns started to come up. Carefully, Shen took an arrow from his quiver and shot one of the suns. To his surprise, it turned into a large crow and fell to the ground. Shen shot very quickly, again and again. Many crows came falling down.

Suddenly, Emperor Yao thought of something. He quickly took one arrow from Shen's quiver and hid it in his own long sleeve.

Finally only one sun was left and the archer reached for his last arrow. It was not there. Shen turned to the emperor in surprise. "Where is my tenth arrow?" he asked. When the wise emperor showed him the arrow, Shen understood. He smiled and bowed.

From that day to this, only one sun rises every morning and crosses the sky. There is only one sun to light and warm the world.

emperor (EM pur ur) an important, powerful ruler, like a king
trembled (TREM buld) shook because of fear or excitement
heavenly (HEV un lee) of or in the heavens or the sky
archer (AR chur) a person who shoots with a bow and arrow
quiver (KWIV ur) a case for holding arrows

Direct Recall

Circle the letter of the choice that best completes each sentence.

1. At the edge of the world was
   a. a wise emperor.   **b.** the Heavenly Archer.   **c.** a certain tree.

2. When the ten suns rose together, the world became too
   a. light.   **b.** hot.   **c.** dark.

3. As each sun was shot, it turned into a
   a. crow.   **b.** arrow.   **c.** star.

4. When Shen reached for his last arrow it was
   a. in his quiver.   **b.** not in his quiver.   **c.** broken.

5. The emperor hid the last arrow
   a. in Shen's quiver.   **b.** in his sleeve.   **c.** under the tree.

Inferential Thinking

Circle the letter of the choice that best completes each item below.

1. When all the suns were in the sky, the people felt
   a. afraid.   **b.** happy.   **c.** sad.

2. The emperor hid the arrow so that
   a. it would not get broken.   **b.** he could give it to Shen.   **c.** one sun would remain in the sky.

3. You can conclude that the next day
   a. ten suns rose again.   **b.** only one sun rose.   **c.** nine suns rose in the sky.

4. Another good title for this story is
   a. "The Wise Emperor."   **b.** "The Ten Crows."   **c.** "Why the Sun Crosses the Sky."

Critical Thinking

1. Which person did more to save the world, Emperor Yao or the Heavenly Archer? Give reasons for your answer.

   _____

2. Old stories often explain why something is true. What does this story explain?

   _____

Vocabulary Development

Using Synonyms

A synonym is a word that means almost the same thing as another word. Using many different words makes your writing better. It makes what you say more interesting, too.

Circle the letter for the synonym of the underlined word. Then write the word you chose in the blank space. Read the sentences again. Do they all make sense?

1. The archer was strong. He was a _____ man.
   a. quick. **b.** brave. **c.** powerful.

2. The people were frightened. The burning sun made them _____.
   a. shy. **b.** fearful. **c.** happy.

3. The emperor was a wise king. He was a _____ ruler.
   a. smart. **b.** careful. **c.** safe.

4. The Heavenly Archer came to aid the people. He tried to _____ them all he could.
   a. help. **b.** food. **c.** protection.

5. The emperor covered the arrow. He _____ it in his sleeve.
   a. moved. **b.** reached. **c.** hid.

6. The emperor's idea was to save one sun. It was a very important _____
   a. thought. **b.** joke. **c.** story.

Test Taking

Read the following passage. Then, complete the items below by filling in the correct choices in the answer grid.

Our sun is a star that is very far from earth. All life on earth depends on it for light and heat. The sun makes all life possible. If the sun's light and heat were to change, all life would be in danger. If the sun were closer to the earth, the earth would get too hot for life to exist. If the sun were farther away, the earth would get too cold.

1. This passage is about how
   a. important the sun is to the earth.
   b. the sun moves across the sky.
   c. hot the sun is in summer.

2. If the sun moved far away, the earth would get too
   a. hot.
   b. cold.
   c. dry.

3. A good title for this passage would be
   a. "The Sun and the Moon."
   b. "Why the Earth Turns."
   c. "How the Sun Helps Us."

	a	b	c		a	b	c		a	b	c
1.	△	△	△	2.	△	△	△	3.	△	△	△

Applying Your Skills

Many beautiful bowls were made long ago in China. The bowls had pictures of people from old stories on them. Decorate a bowl of your own. Choose a part of the story you liked best. Draw your picture on the bowl.

THE COLORS IN YOUR GARDEN

Spring is the time of year when all the colorful flowers start to bloom. Some scientists say that long ago, springtime may not have been so colorful.

- How many different kinds of flowers do you know?
- How do bees pollinate flowers?

Some scientists think that millions of years ago, most flowers were either green or white. They think that flowers of other colors were very rare.

Scientists have an idea that explains why there are now flowers of so many different colors. Their idea is that bees were responsible for the many different colors of flowers.

Here's how the idea goes. A flower must be pollinated for its seeds to grow. Pollen must be carried from the part of the flower where it is made to the part where the seeds are. The pollen makes it possible for the seeds of the flower to grow into the same kind of flower.

Millions of years ago, only the wind carried pollen. This was a very risky way for the pollen to reach flowers. The wind had to blow the pollen in just the right direction. Because the wind's direction was changeable, many kinds of flowers were never pollinated. Those flowers never grew again.

Later, insects became the carriers of pollen. It happened because the insects came to sip nectar from the flowers. While they were inside the flowers, the insects got pollen on their legs. Then, they flew from plant to plant carrying the pollen.

The most common nectar-eating insects were bees. Unlike most insects, bees can see certain colors. They can see blue, yellow, and violet. Perhaps, bees liked flowers with these colors more than they liked green or white ones. Perhaps, the bees sipped nectar from them more often and, in doing that, pollinated them. In that way, the green and white flowers were less likely to be pollinated than the flowers with other colors. Slowly, over millions of years, there began to be more flowers that were not just green or white.

Just think of it! Because bees can see certain colors, we can now make beautiful bouquets of many, differently colored flowers.

pollinate (POL uh nayt)   to carry pollen to the place where flower's seeds are in a flower
rare (RAYR)   not often seen or found
pollen (POL uhn)   the yellow powder near the center of a flower
nectar (NEK tuhr)   a sweet liquid found in flowers that is used by bees to make honey
bouquet (boh KAY)   a bunch of cut flowers

Direct Recall

Circle the letter of the choice that best completes each sentence.

1. Some scientists think that millions of years ago, most flowers were
   a. green or white.   b. bigger than they are now.   c. purple and blue.

2. They think that flowers of other colors were
   a. rare.   b. common.   c. everywhere.

3. Millions of years ago, pollen was carried only by the
   a. birds.   b. clouds.   c. wind.

4. The most common nectar-eating insects were
   a. flies.   b. bees.   c. spiders.

5. Bees can see the colors blue, yellow, and
   a. violet.   b. red.   c. white.

Inferential Thinking

Circle the letter of the choice that best completes each item below.

1. Some scientists think that
   a. colored flowers are nicer than white ones.
   b. bees helped more flowers of different colors to grow.
   c. pollen was invented by bees.

2. Bees went to the flowers that were not green or white because
   a. those flowers smelled better.
   b. their colors got the bees' attention.
   c. the bees couldn't see red.

3. Today there are many different color flowers because
   a. bees pollinated them.
   b. bees hated them.
   c. people liked them for bouquets.

4. Another good title for this selection might be
   a. "Why There Are So Many Different Color Flowers Today."
   b. "How Bees Live."
   c. "Nectar from the Flowers."

Critical Thinking

1. If there were no bees, what colors would flowers be today? Give reasons for your answer.

   _____

2. How do you think that scientists found out that bees can see different colors?

   _____

Memory Technique

Taking Notes to Remember Facts

One way to help remember what you are reading is to take notes. To take notes, write down the important ideas in the passage. Words like *the* or *and* are not important to the idea. Read the following sentences:

Bees are able to see different colors. They find green or white flowers less interesting than flowers of other colors.

Your notes might be:

_____

_____

_____

Now try it yourself. Read the following passage and take notes on it.

There is only one color of flower that scientists think we cannot thank bees for. That color is red. Bees cannot see red. Therefore, scientists think we have other insects to thank for red flowers.

Notes: _____

_____

_____

Test Taking

Read the following passage. Then complete the items below by filling in the correct choices in the answer grid.

> Bees are smarter than many people think. When a bee finds flowers, it goes back to its hive. It tells the other bees about the flowers. It tells them by dancing and singing because bees can't talk. The dance tells where the flowers are and how far away they are. The song tells if there is a lot of nectar in the flowers. After the dance and song, every bee in the hive can find the flowers.

1. When a bee finds some flowers, it
   a. takes a nap in them.
   b. goes back to its hive.
   c. starts making honey.

2. Which of the following is not true?
   a. The bee's dance tells what color the flowers are.
   b. The bee's dance tells where the flowers are
   c. The bee's dance tells how far away the flowers are.

3. The bee dances and sings so that other bees will
   a. find their way home.
   b. will find the flowers.
   c. think it is smart.

	a	b	c		a	b	c		a	b	c
1.	△	△	△	2.	△	△	△	3.	△	△	△

Applying Your Skills

Read the clues below, then fill in the crossword puzzle with the correct words from the box.

bouquet	color	rare	green	pollen	nectar	bee	pollinate

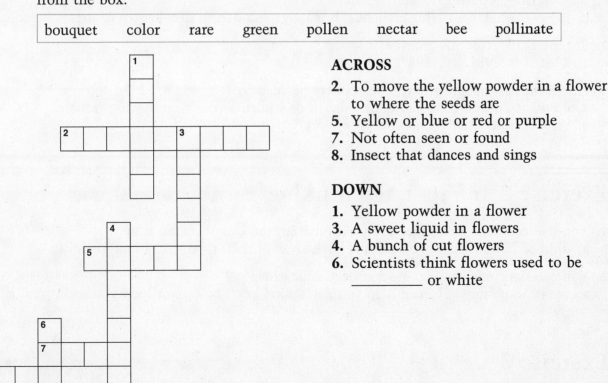

ACROSS

2. To move the yellow powder in a flower to where the seeds are
5. Yellow or blue or red or purple
7. Not often seen or found
8. Insect that dances and sings

DOWN

1. Yellow powder in a flower
3. A sweet liquid in flowers
4. A bunch of cut flowers
6. Scientists think flowers used to be _____ or white

Review Exercise 1

A PROMISE

Directions: Read the following paragraphs and then answer the questions below. For Exercises 1 and 2, circle the letter of the best answer. For Exercise 3, write the answer in the space provided.

In 1981, a businessman name Eugene Lang did a surprising thing. He made a promise to 61 sixth-graders in New York City. He said he would pay to send each one of them to college. All they had to do was stay in school.

Many students in the United States do not finish high school. This is especially true of students who come from poor families and live in big cities. Eugene Lang wanted to give a few children a good reason to stay in school. It turned out he did more than that.

People around the country read in newspapers about Eugene Lang's promise. Other wealthy people decided that they would also do what Eugene Lang had done. They went to schools near their homes. They promised young students to pay for their college educations if they just stayed in school.

Eugene Lang's students are now ready to go to college. Eugene Lang and others like him are trying to help poor children have greater opportunities in the future.

Exercise 1 Direct Recall

1. Eugene Lang promised 61 sixth-graders
   a. to pay to send them to high school.   **b.** to pay to send them to college.   **c.** to stay in school.

2. Eugene Lang made his promise in
   a. 1961.   **b.** 1981.   **c.** 1987.

3. Other wealthy people around the country decided to
   a. do what Eugene Lang had done.   **b.** tutor students who were having trouble.
   c. visit Eugene Lang's school in New York City.

Exercise 2 Inferential Thinking

1. You can conclude that other people copied Eugene Lang because they
   a. did not like his idea.   **b.** did not have ideas of their own.   **c.** liked his idea.

2. You can conclude that having a college education
   a. is not important.   **b.** can help you get a good job.   **c.** cannot help you get a good job.

Exercise 3 Critical Thinking

Why do you think Eugene Lang decided to make his promise?

THE WAR OF THE WORLDS

Directions: Read the following paragraphs and then answer the questions below. For Exercises 1 and 2, circle the letter of the best answer. For Exercise 3, write the answer in the space provided.

"On October 30, 1938, men from Mars invaded the planet Earth." No, it didn't really happen. But thousands of people listening to their radios that night thought that Martians had taken over the planet.

It was a night that will always be remembered in the history of radio. People were listening to a Sunday night radio show called Mercury Theatre. That night a play based on the book *The War of the Worlds* by H. G. Wells was being presented. The play was written in the form of a news bulletin. Thousands of people heard, "We interrupt this broadcast. . . ." They believed that what followed was true. They believed that monsters from Mars had invaded New Jersey and were taking over the planet. But it was really only a play.

People ran out of their houses to try to escape from the Martian invaders. There was panic everywhere.

Exercise 1 Direct Recall

1. A play was presented on the radio based on the book
   a. *Men from Mars.*   **b.** *The War of the Worlds.*   **c.** *Mercury Theatre.*

2. The play was written in the form of a
   a. comedy.   **b.** newspaper article.   **c.** news bulletin.

3. Many people believed that monsters from Mars had invaded
   a. New Jersey.   **b.** New York.   **c.** New Hampshire.

Exercise 2 Inferential Thinking

1. There was panic everywhere because many people believed that what was happening in the radio play
   a. was actually happening.   **b.** was not true.   **c.** was fantastic.

2. Another good title for this selection is
   a. Radio Shows.   **b.** Invasion from Mars.   **c.** The Planet Earth.

Critical Thinking

How do you think so many people could mistake a play for something real?

JIM THORPE—ALL-AMERICAN

Directions: Read the following paragraphs and then answer the questions below. For Exercises 1 and 2, circle the letter of the best answer. For Exercise 3, write the answer in the space provided.

Jim Thorpe was born in 1888 in what is now Oklahoma but was then called Indian Territory. His grandfather was a famous chief named Black Hawk. Jim Thorpe may have been the greatest all-around athlete in American history.

Jim Thorpe played football in high school and college. He was named to the All-American football team two years in a row. He later played professional football for 15 years.

Not only did Thorpe play football, he also played professional baseball. He was an outfielder for the New York Giants, the Cincinnati Reds, and the Boston Braves.

In addition to being a great football and baseball player, Thorpe was an outstanding runner. He won two major races in the 1912 Olympic Games.

In 1950, a poll named Jim Thorpe the greatest all-around athlete of the 20th century. It's easy to see why.

Exercise 1 Direct Recall

1. Jim Thorpe was born in what is now
   a. Oklahoma.   **b.** Indian Territory.   **c.** New York.

2. Jim Thorpe played football
   a. only in high school.   **b.** only in college.   **c.** in high school, in college, and professionally.

3. Jim Thorpe played baseball as
   a. an infielder.   **b.** an outfielder.   **c.** a runner.

Exercise 2 Inferential Thinking

1. The main idea of this selection is that Jim Thorpe was
   a. an Indian.   **b.** a football player.   **c.** an outstanding athlete.

2. Which statement is an opinion?
   a. Jim Thorpe played football.   **b.** Jim Thorpe was on the All-American team.
   c. Jim Thorpe was a great football player.

Exercise 3 Critical Thinking

What do you think it takes to become an outstanding athlete?

THE SONG OF THE PLOW

Directions: Read the following paragraphs and then answer the questions below. For Exercises 1 and 2, circle the letter of the best answer. For Exercise 3, write the answer in the space provided.

Farming was difficult in the early days of our country. In the east, the soil was sometimes poor and rocky. A farm family had to work full-time just to feed themselves. So, a lot of farmers moved west to the Great Plains. The farmland there was the best they had ever seen. They thought it would be easier to grow more food.

When they got to the plains, there was a big problem. The soil was *too* good. The plows could not get through the thick ground. The soil of the Great Plains was so heavy and rich it stuck to the farmers' plows. Many people tried to solve this problem. No one could do it.

Finally, a young blacksmith named John Deere decided he would try. He took a piece of the best steel he could find. He thought about the shape that was needed. Then carefully, he hammered it into that shape. When he was finished, he tested it. The farmers came from all around to watch. The new plow worked! It cut through the soil easily. Also, it cleaned itself as it moved. Now, the farmers could plant crops in the rich soil of the Great Plains. They could feed their families and perhaps have food left to sell.

The steel plow made a humming sound as it went through the soil. People called this sound "The Song of the Plow."

Exercise 1 Direct Recall

1. The problem with the soil of the Great Plains was that it was too
   a. rocky.　**b.** good.　**c.** poor.

2. John Deere was a
   a. farmer.　**b.** soldier.　**c.** blacksmith.

3. The new plow could
   a. pull up trees.　**b.** clean itself.　**c.** plant seeds.

Exercise 2 Inferential Thinking

1. Farmers moved to the Great Plains because they heard that
   a. the land was rich.　**b.** the land was beautiful.　**c.** they did not want to work.

2. Probably the farmers thought that the song of the plow was
   a. too loud.　**b.** a wonderful noise.　**c.** a big problem.

Exercise 3 Critical Thinking

Did the new plow change city peoples' lives? Give reasons for your answer.

THE WOLF AND THE DOG, BY AESOP

Directions: Read the following story and then answer the questions below. For Exercises 1 and 2, circle the letter of the best answer. For Exercise 3, write the answer in the space provided.

A poor and hungry wolf met a plump and well-fed dog. The wolf greeted the dog as a long-lost member of the family. He told the dog how well he looked.

"That's more than I can say for you," the dog said. He looked sadly at the dirty, hungry wolf.

"Times have been hard, cousin," said the wolf, "But I can see that *you* aren't hungry."

"That is because my master takes care of me," said the dog. "He gives me plenty to eat."

"Do you think your master would give me food?" asked the wolf. "I am really hungry."

"Come along," said the dog. "There is plenty of work and food for two."

As they walked along, the wolf noticed something hanging around the dog's neck and asked about it. The dog told him it was a collar. The wolf asked what the collar was for.

"It is so my master can attach a chain to it and keep me nearby if he wants to."

"Thank you and goodbye," said the wolf. "I'd much rather be poor and hungry forever than be chained up like a slave."

Exercise 1 Direct Recall

1. The wolf calls the dog
   a. a friend.   b. a cousin.   c. an enemy.

2. The dog said there was
   a. enough work and food for two.   b. enough work but not enough food.
   c. not enough room.

3. The dog wore a collar
   a. to look pretty.   b. to let people know his name.   c. so his master could chain him.

Exercise 2 Inferential Thinking

1. The dog was well fed because
   a. he knew how to hunt.   b. he was a good worker.   c. his master was very rich.

2. The wolf liked being
   a. a slave.   b. hungry.   c. free.

Exercise 3 Critical Thinking

Which two of the following three would you rather have:

> plenty of food
> freedom
> a warm place to sleep

Give reasons for your answer.

THE SLOWEST MAMMAL

Directions: Read the following paragraphs and then answer the questions below. For Exercises 1 and 2, circle the letter of the best answer. For Exercise 3, write the answer in the space provided.

How would you like to live your whole life in just one place? Well, the tree sloth does. The tree sloth almost never goes anywhere. It certainly never goes anywhere in a hurry. It spends most of its life hanging upside down from a tree branch. It even walks upside down.

The tree sloth has long, hooked claws and uses them to hold on to tree branches. Sloths hold on to branches so hard that it is almost impossible to pull them off.

Sloths even sleep on branches. They hang upside down and hold on with all four feet. They sleep about eighteen hours a day, yet they always seem to be tired. That is why the word *slothful* is used to describe lazy people.

You may wonder how a sloth gets its food. Here's how: it slowly picks off the leaves and fruit that it can reach from where it is hanging. After it has eaten everything within reach, it s-l-o-w-l-y moves, little by little, to another branch. Then, it starts all over again.

Watching a sloth is not the most exciting way to spend your time.

Exercise 1 Direct Recall

1. Sloths walk
   a. rapidly. **b.** upside down. **c.** sideways.

2. *Slothful* means
   a. lazy. **b.** harmful. **c.** quick-tempered.

3. The sloth uses its claws to
   a. run from danger. **b.** attack other animals. **c.** hold onto tree branches.

Exercise 2 Inferential Thinking

1. You can conclude that sloths live
   a. where it is always cool or cold. **b.** where it is always warm or hot.
   c. where there are trees.

2. Another good title for this selection is
   a. An Upside-Down Life. **b.** Learning to Hang Upside Down. **c.** From Branch to Branch.

Exercise 3 Critical Thinking

Would you like to have a sloth for a pet? Give reasons for your answer.

GLOSSARY

A

abolitionist (ab uh LISH uhn ist) *n.* a person who favored ending slavery

adventures (ad VEN churz) *n.* unusual, exciting, or dangerous experiences

advice (ad VYS) *n.* an opinion about what someone should do

amazed (uh MAYZD) *v.* greatly surprised; astonished

amazement (uh MAYZ munt) *n.* great surprise

ancestors (AN ses turs) *n.* early animals from which later kinds have developed

ancient (AYN shunt) *adj.* from long ago

angrily (AN grih lee) *adv.* in a way that shows anger

antlers (ANT lurz) *n.* branched horns of animals of the deer family

archer (AR chur) *n.* a person who shoots with a bow and arrow

asteroid (AS tuh roid) *n.* small rocky body that revolves around the sun

astronaut (AS truh naut) *n.* a person who is trained to fly a spaceship

astronomers (uh STRAHN uh murz) *n.* scientists who study the stars

audience (AW dee uns) *n.* people gathered to hear or watch something, such as a vaudeville act, a movie, or a play.

avoid (uh VOID) *v.* stay away from

axis (AK sis) *n.* a real or imaginary line around which something, such as the earth, turns, or seems to turn

B

basin (BAYS un) *n.* a round, shallow bowl for holding liquids

behavior (bih HAYV yur) *n.* way of acting

billion (BIL yun) *n.* a thousand million; 1,000,000,000

bouquet (boh KAY) *n.* a bunch of cut flowers

boycott (BOI kot) *n.* refusal to buy a product or use a service

breed (BREED) *n.* a special kind of animal or plant

buffaloes (BUF uh lohz) *n.* wild oxen

C

campfire (KAMP fyr) *n.* an outdoor fire, as at a campsite

centuries (SEN chur eez) *n.* periods of one hundred years

champion (CHAM pee un) *adj.* the best

chemical (KEM ih kul) *n.* a substance that can produce an effect by itself or in combination with another substance

collage (kuh LAHZH) *n.* a work of art made by pasting materials on a surface

comedian (kuh MEE dee un) *n.* an actor who plays comic parts

complain (kum PLAYN) *v.* say that something is wrong; to find fault

complicated (KOM pluh kayt id) *adj.* not simple; intricate

conditions (kun DISH unz) *n.* the way things are

confusion (kun FYOO zhun) *n.* being mixed up or bewildered

congratulate (kun GRAT yoo layt) *v.* to tell a person you are pleased with what he or she has done

controls (kun TROHLZ) *n.* the system for operating an airplane

courage (KUR ij) *n.* bravery

courses (KAWR sez) *n.* different parts of a meal

coyote (ky OHT ee) *n.* a small wolf

created (kree AY tid) *v.* brought into being; made

creature (KREE chur) *n.* a living being

criticize (KRIT uh syz) *v.* say bad things about; find fault with

crops (KROPS) *n.* plants grown to be used

crunch (KRUNCH) *n.* crackling sound

custom (KUS tum) *n.* a usual way of doing things

D

dangerous (DAYN jer us) *adj.* full of danger; risky

digits (DIJ its) *n.* the main parts of hands and feet; fingers, thumbs, and toes

dignity (DIG nih tee) *n.* a noble, stately, honorable manner

dinosaur (DY nuh SAWR) *n.* a large animal that lived millions of years ago

disgusted (dis GUST id) *v.*   feeling sick, as from a bad smell

double (DUB l) *v.*   become twice as big as usual

dough (DOH) *n.*   flour, water, and yeast for making bread

downstream (DOUN streem) *n.*   in a direction or place toward the lower part of a stream or river

E

editor (ED uh tur) *n.*   a person who get books ready to be published

election (ih LEK shun) *n.*   the process of choosing people by voting

elk (ELK) *n.*   a large deer

emperor (EM pur ur) *n.*   an important, powerful ruler, like a king

empire (EM pyr) *n.*   a large area of land ruled by one person or one country

endangered (en DAYN jerd) *adj.*   unprotected; to be in peril

energy (EN ur jee) *n.*   power to do work

equipment (i KWIP munt) *n.*   things that are needed when making a long trip

exactly (ig ZAKT lee) *adv.*   precisely; just the same as

exaggerating (ig ZAJ uh rayt ing) *v.*   making something seem more than it is

examined (eg ZAM und) *v.*   looked at carefully

expensive (ik SPEN siv) *adj.*   having a high price; costing a lot

experiment (ik SPER uh munt) *v.*   to try something; to test out

experts (EKS purts) *n.*   people who have much special knowledge and experience

extinct (eks TINGT) *adj.*   die out; no longer exist

F

fare (FAIR) *n.*   the cost of a ride

fast-food (FAST FOOD) *adj.*   specializing in food that is prepared and served quickly

feast (FEEST) *n.*   a large, fancy meal

features (FEE churz) *n.*   parts of the face, such as the eyes, the nose, and the mouth

flexible (FLEK suh bul) *adj.*   able to bend easily

flippers (FLIP urz) *n.*   the broad, flat limbs on some animals, such as seals and penguins

G

gather (GATH ur) *v.*   get and bring together

generous (JEN ur us) *adj.*   willing to give or share

gliding (GLYD ing) *v.*   moving smoothly

graciously (GRAY shus lee) *adv.*   with courtesy and kindness

greedy (GREE dee) *adj.*   selfish

H

habitat (HAB i tat) *n.*   the place where an animal lives or grows

heavenly (HEV un lee) *adj.*   of or in the heavens or the sky

hero (HEER oh) *n.*   the main good character in a story

honor (AHN ur) *n.*   great respect

hut (HUT) *n.*   small, plain dwelling

I

imaginations (ih maj uh NAY shunz) *n.*   power of forming pictures in the mind

in-laws (IN lawz) *n.*   relatives by marriage; family of one's husband or wife

influence (IN floo uns) *v.*   have an effect on; change

invasion (in VAY zhun) *n.*   an attack

invented (in VEN tid) *v.*   made or created for the first time

invention (in VEN shun) *v.*   the act of thinking out or making something that did not exist before

islanders (EYE lund urz) *n.*   people living on islands

K

knowledge (NOL ij) *n.*   information that is known

L

labor (LAY bur) *n.*   work

launched (LAUNCHT) *v.*   pushed off

league (LEEG) *n.*   a group of sports teams that play against one another

legend (LEJ und) *n.*   ancient story

lightning (LYT ning) *n.*   a flash of light in the sky caused by electricity passing between clouds or between a cloud and the earth

liquid (LIK wid) *n.*   a substance that flows freely, like water

M

manufactured (man yuh FAK churd) *adj.* made, especially by machines

marine biologists (muh REEN by OL uh jists) *n.* scientists who study sea plants and animals

master (MAS tur) *v.* become good at

mating (MAYT ing) *adj.* pairing of animals to produce offspring

medicine (MED uh sin) *n.* the science of treating and preventing disease

N

narcissus (nar SIS us) *n.* the name of a white or yellow flower

naturally (NAT choo ral ee) *adv.* in a natural manner; by nature

nectar (NEK tuhr) *n.* a sweet liquid found in flowers that is used by bees to make honey

nonsense (NON sens) *n.* foolish behavior, actions, or ideas

O

observatory (ub ZER vuh tawr ee) *n.* a building that houses telescopes

opposable (uh POH zuh bul) *adj.* able to be placed opposite from and to touch the fingers of the hand of which it is a part

optimism (OP tuh miz um) *n.* the belief that everything will be fine

orbit (OR bit) *n.* the path followed by a satellite; a single trip by a satellite around a body in space

P

penalties (PEN uhl teez) *n.* punishments

performer (pur FAWRM ur) *n.* a person who entertains on stage in front of an audience

Peru (puh ROO) *n.* a country on the west coast of South America

phosphorus (FOS fur us) *n.* a chemical that can make fire

photographs (FOHT uh grafs) *n.* pictures taken with a camera

pilot (PY lut) *n.* a person who operates an airplane

piloted (PY lut id) *v.* acted as the pilot; operated an airplane

pioneer (py uh NEER) *n.* one of the first people to settle a region; a person who leads the way

plains (PLAYNZ) *n.* large, flat expanses of land

policy (POL uh see) *n.* a plan or course of action

pollen (POL uhn) *n.* the yellow powder near the center of a flower

pollinate (POL uh nayt) *v.* to carry pollen to the place where seeds are in a flower

polluted (poh LOO ted) *adj.* not healthy; poisoned

population (pop yuh LAY shun) *n.* number of people living in a place

pottery (POT ur ee) *n.* objects made from soft clay and hardened by heat

prehistoric (pree his TAWR ik) *adj.* of the time before people wrote history

prey (PRAY) *n.* an animal hunted for food by another animal

private (PRY vit) *adj.* just for oneself

profession (pruh FESH un) *n.* a job that requires special training

published (PUB lisht) *v.* printed and offered for sale

Q

quiver (KWIV ur) *n.* a case for holding arrows

R

rabbi (RAB eye) *n.* a teacher or leader in the Jewish religion

radiation (ray dee AY shun) *n.* energy given off in the form of rays

rare (RAYR) *adj.* not often seen or found

reelected (ree ih LEKT id) *v.* elected again

reflection (rih FLEK shun) *n.* an image given back to one, as from a mirror

related (rih LAYT id) *adj.* being of the same family or kind

reluctantly (ree LUK tant lee) *adv.* not wanting to

revolve (rih VOLV) *v.* move around in an orbit

reward (rih WARD) *n.* something given for doing something

S

satellite (SAT ul yt) *n.* an object that goes around a body in space

satisfied (SAT is fyd) *v.* contented; pleased

scattered (SKAT urd) *v.* spread out

scientist (SY un tist) *n.* an expert in a science

section (SEK shun) *n.* part

sedition (sih DISH un) *n.* speech or writing that makes people angry with their government

sentenced (SEN tunst) *v.* given as punishment

servant (SUR vunt) *n.* a person who works in someone else's home

service (SUR vis) *n.* useful work

sickness (SIK nis) *n.* the condition of being sick; disease

sighted (SYT id) *adj.* able to see

silently (SY lunt lee) *adv.* without making a sound

single (SING gul) *adj.* only one

solo (SOH loh) *adv.* alone

stored (STORD) *v.* put away for future use

strangest (STRAYNJ est) *adj.* most different or peculiar; oddest

successfully (suk SES ful lee) *adv.* with a good result

Supreme Court (suh PREEM kort) *n.* the highest court in the United States

survive (sur VYV) *v.* to last through a dangerous time

T

Tahiti (tuh HEET ee) *n.* an island in the South Pacific

take-out (TAYK out) *adj.* specializing in food that is to be taken out and eaten somewhere else

tale (TAYL) *n.* a story

tennis (TEN is) *n.* a game played by hitting a ball over a net to an opponent

tepee (TEE pee) *n.* a tent made of animal skins and shaped like a cone

terrified (TER uh fyd) *v.* very frightened

theories (THEE uh reez) *n.* explanations of how or why something happens

trained (TRAYND) *v.* taught

training (TRAYN ing) *v.* teaching; education

treated (TREET id) *v.* acted toward

trembled (TREM buld) *v.* shook because of fear or excitement

tremendous (trih MEN dus) *adj.* very, very big

U

unhealthy (un HEL thee) *adj.* not good for living things

universe (YOO nuh vurs) *n.* the whole world

upstream (UP streem) *n.* in a direction or place toward the higher part of a stream or river

V

varsity (VAHR suh tee) *n.* the main team that plays for a school in a competition

vaudeville (VAWD vil) *n.* a stage show with songs, dances, and comic acts

villain (VIL un) *n.* a wicked person in a story

W

waterway (WAW tur way) *n.* a water route that ships and boats can travel through

woo (WOO) *v.* try to win the love of